SIGNS OF THE TIMES

Gaither Stewart

ISBN: 978-93-88319-47-8

First Edition: 2020
Rs. 200/-

Cyberwit.net
HIG 45 Kaushambi Kunj, Kalindipuram
Allahabad - 211011 (U.P.) India
http://www.cyberwit.net
Tel: +(91) 9415091004
E-mail: info@cyberwit.net

Printed at Thomson Press India Limited.

Contents

AUTHOR'S PREFACE

Novelists can easily agree that fiction offers true and realistic history because it shows the turmoil and conflicts that real people experience in their daily lives in a way that pure history does not. Fiction shows not only what people of the real world experience but also what they feel. Although my fiction contains pieces of history and details about the places where things happen, my major attention goes to fictional people who make history both true and realistic. What people feel is fundamental to my conception of fiction. The assorted characters you will meet in the stories in SIGNS OF THE TIMES show unabashedly their feelings about their lives: their general absence of certainties, their incurable malaise and their unrelenting loneliness as they tentatively make their way toward their destinies.

Many historians perceive of history itself as a determining force that individual lives merely illustrate. I agree only partially. History presents the facts in a certain manner and from a certain point of view. Fiction offers the reality for which most fiction writers strive. Fiction writers can reconstruct events as well as historians but they may also put real people in imaginary situations in a way historians cannot. Fred Weinstein in his *History and Theory* writes that while non-fiction gives you the facts, fiction gives you the truth. History tells you what happened; fiction tells you how it felt to the people who lived it. Fiction shows how people attempt to find and understand themselves. Contrary to history, fiction shows how the times in which people live shape them and how people seeking autonomy face the challenges of their times, and thus how people also shape their times.

While the history that people have lived challenges the imaginative capacity of historians to account for it, it is fiction that can offer the heterogeneity and discontinuity that history written by historians cannot. (Weinstein) I believe that fiction can bring readers closer to the subjective perceptions of people in history. As Nicola Chiaromonte writes in *Paradox of History*: *Only in fiction and the imaginary can we learn something real about individual experience.*

Only in the great sweep of epochs can people be reduced to mere "illustrators" of history. Decades ago I was fixated on the determining role of 'historic Rome'; today, as I come to know the historical significance of my adoptive home city, ancient Rome emerges as proof that *pure* historicism has no heart. How can it have a heart when, as Napoleon said, "*It marches with the victors.*"

The fictional stories in this collection also contain partially historical autobiography in the sense of Montaigne's words that "my writings and I are one." In fact, since I the writer am often also the narrator within the story, I am in symbiosis with the protagonist and/or narrator. So, since the stories in SIGNS OF THE TIMES are conceived as a world story, I have permitted myself flashbacks of my own past. And as a rule the characters conclude that many things change less than we sometimes believe.

These stories are also marked by much introspection, in which the characters think and articulate their ideas in order to reduce the gap between reality and the world of fantasy. Remembrances play a major role in these stories: remembrances—true or invented—as do politics and history which also are both true and invented.

Alternating between fiction and personal history, I offer a combination of political thought, history, fictional fantasy, and autobiography. Liberation from the restrictions of genre, linearity, time and space opens new territories for the writer who encounters scattered fragments of him/herself in his/her free passage from one genre to the other—fictionalizing real historical-political occurrences or transforming fantasies into reality—while, at the same time, not sacrificing truth for effect or genre.

Literary fiction requires a linguistic source. I have lived in non-English-speaking countries my entire adult life and now for the last decades in an Italian-speaking milieu in which little English is spoken with the result that I sometimes tend to invent vocabulary or imitate the English I hear, read or imagine.

The inquiring reader might wonder about my obsessions. My relationship with the opposite sex, as in the story *Harriet, Harriet,* results in stories based on a powerful erotic drive or stories in which romantic relationships easily become obsessions. And thus my attention to the problematics and uncertainties of personal relationships.

These stories are imbuedwith the familiar topos of alienation: deracination and the search for one's real place. The protagonist of the last tale, *The Scent of Mahogany,* presents himself as a coward seeking redemption. Such themes are not intellectual playthings; they are serious issues for the writer. My original alienation stems from what I might sum up as 'boredom with the routine and the indifference of my original homeland'. I left them behind. I believe there is more to be had "out there with *the others*" of the world to whom many of my fellow countrymen still seem indifferent. Not that I or my heroes are particularly gregarious sorts. Perhaps because I tend to be a lonely person, my personal alienation and uprootedness transform my life into a search for myself and for a new place as an ersatz for my ur-home.

However, after an initial love affair with romantic Italy, I met here the same indifference that I had mistaken for the mystery of that land's diversity which the greatest of poets have futilely tried to unravel. My characters conclude that those like the great Goethe have been no more successful than Italy's own peoples, who still today fail to understand themselves. Moreover, I have discovered that indifference is also an all-European sickness, a disease that is corroding European society as it has that of my former homeland: looking away from the losers in life symbolized by the rejection of the flood of refugees; the closing of eyes to social injustice; the pervasive abyss between rich and poor; the resurgence of Fascism; the popular indifference to public corruption; and the general indifference to war. Indifference has come to mean 'no difference.'

From awareness of the general indifference emerges a perturbing consciousness of a missing quality in today's human beings: respect for their fellowmen. Though I do not often use the word *respect*, it is a major driving force in my social critique as seen in my concern for what I call *the others*. The *others out there* people my pessimistic world outlook.

The Euro-American spirit is not universalistic, while the past is its enemy, its unwanted traveling companion whose ghosts are audible in the moments of bursts of truncated laughter. America's ghosts mourn for the things lost within that irretrievable time, ghosts condemned to wander through space in search of those lost things. What fleeting meaning to give to the deceit of the obligatory pledges to respect the symbols of the myth and to a society in which educated and superficially intelligent people bow down to the god of lies? A society in which the quality of loyalty remains intact even though the objects of that loyalty—the persons and ideas—have become disloyal to its worshippers. Like lost empires—British, Hapsburgian or Aztec—ghostly voices from the past resurface from the imperialistic underworld and merge into some form of consciousness. Secrets from that past do not remain forever secrets, one of my protagonists thinks. Everything in our world, every object and every person, point back toward the revelation of the mystery of existence and its one common origin. Thus everything is a copy of something else which is a replica of a replica of a copy of an original as in the story *Melancholy.* Existence becomes repetition—and nothing is lost.

Therefore, my characters search for something different. Although I accept that I am locked in the white race for which I hold little hope, my personae want to be 'out there' where I believe we all should be. In the same way the characters in these stories may never find that which they are seeking; they may never even find the perfect replacement for what they think of as their permanent place, somewhere beyond their obsessions for that one place and one person that will be the end of the search—the result of the injudicious weight I, the writer, give to place. I respect the past but like the narrator-hero of *Coyoacan-Place of the Coyotes,* I never intend a return to it.

The "Source"—so-named by the author of this story)

HARRIET, HARRIET

What might have been and what has been
Point to one end, which is always present.
Footfalls echo in the memory
Down the passage which we did not take....

T.S. Eliot

After Alessandra killed herself with barbiturates in a countryside house near Oxford, a psychically transformed Karl Rasch renounced a brilliant academic career in England and returned once and for all to his native Germany. Though he had a German father, a German mother, a German passport and had visited there often, Karl had never actually lived there before. "Return" was a euphemism for discovery: his aim was to re-discover Germany. So, at thirty-two years he set about building a new life in a new country. He had an inheritance, a profession, an apartment in Munich, new friends and he soon found the ideal job for him as a teacher in a German Gymnasium. Karl felt rejuvenated; he was starting his new life with a mission that occupied both his earthly body and his spiritual soul. Above all, he hoped it would erase his weighty memory of memories of Alessandra. At the same time, however, he perceived the co-existence in himself of stormy heights and contradictory desires: love and sadness, fears of today, and bright hopes for the morrow.

Though he disliked academic life as such, Karl loved teaching. With his superior qualifications, he secured a position at the city's most exclusive Gymnasium as the teacher of a course he himself designed: he tailored "*the Humanities*" for thirteenth school year students and had wide freedom to determine the course subject matter which, he felt, reflected the School Board's appreciation of the caliber of his scholarship. So he was at first startled though not displeased by the disproportionate number of nineteen-year-old young ladies who signed up for *the Humanities*.

A few details about Karl's physical features are necessary here. So, I will describe him in a few quick strokes and have done with it. Karl Maria Rasch was tall and slim with thick dark hair, the high cheekbones and forehead of his Prussian father, the large sparkling wide-set light blue eyes of his Rhineland mother. He was well-dressed in an innate sloppy sort of way which was part of his charm. So that when he stood before the class theorizing on the existence of the soul, his look fastened on one or the other of his students, his piercing eyes entranced the young ladies each of whom seemed to feel special and the center of the world. The school board members came to call it the Karl Rasch Effect.

The girls' attraction to him was nothing new for Karl. Women had always found him fascinating and for as long as he could remember women had been a major part of his life. The quality Karl loved most about women was what he considered their instinct for true beauty. Not the superficial beauty of face and body they saw in him, but soul beauty, as he called it. For that reason, he said, he loved women passionately, which he believed accounted for their attraction to him. Even his mother had favored him among his siblings. Karl was convinced that women loved him also because he truly understood them … and was not afraid of them as many men seemed to be. Moreover, he believed in love. And love, he thought, was not for the weak. The weak could only be loved; to truly love another requires open-minded generosity and moral character. Love was selflessness.

When envious friends asked for his advice on their relationships with women, he answered with the cliché: "Don't ever ask a woman what women are like."

The downside of his easy-going relationship with the opposite sex was that he wandered through life from the loving arms of one woman to the embrace of another, loving them all and being loved in return, but also breaking hearts and having his own broken along the way. His ordered world had been convulsed a couple of years earlier when after his sudden break-up with Sara, his best male friend in England had remarked that he seemed to enjoy using his charm to make women love him for the joy of then leaving them; Karl broke violently with Harold, too, aware however that he was in the wrong for at break-up time he too had wondered if some suppressed part of his past was not responsible. So at around that time, he became conscious of an unarticulated battle in his subconscious between his conscience and his self-esteem. "But Karl, what about all those women in your life?" insisted his closest Munich colleague. He and Manfred were sitting at a rough wooden table in a beer garden across the river. A half-liter of light beer and an empty shot glass of a vodka-like Dornkaat stood in front of each. It was their second round.

On this late afternoon of a beautiful October day, a light southern breeze was blowing through the chestnut trees and pines of the English

Garden. The quiet, tenacious day drinkers had gone, and it was still early for the noisy evening crowd; they were nearly alone with the waitresses.

"You loved them, and then you, er, you left them … or they left you," the historian Manfred said hesitantly. "What about the pain and the grief? Didn't you suffer when one left you? *Donnerwetter*! I think I would suffer too much to live that uncertain kind of love life. Makes you sound like a gigolo of the spirit."

"Well, love doesn't come for free, that's certain."

"Yes, one or the other always suffers more from a separation," Manfred insisted. "So it's a case of you or her."

"I never thought of it that way. Still, except for Alessandra, I have few regrets … maybe because each love was so limited in time. But admittedly my love has never seemed to bring anyone lasting happiness, you know, maybe because I never made any major sacrifices for those I loved. For me, the first rapture of falling in love is pure joy. Something real. That's what counts. That's what I look forward to. It's never painful. I've never suffered the 'pangs of love' of love songs. The pain of separation, yes. What's hard for me is not to be loved. But then I've learned to accept the break-up pain as the price of love."

"Strange world you live in, Karl. Funny that you seldom speak of a specific woman. Or why you loved her." Manfred drained the last drop of beer, raised his hand, and called to the approaching waitress who knew her drinkers' desires before they did: "*Noch zwei, bitte*". Then he added: "Seems you were loving yourself more than the loved one."

"Maybe you're right. To some extent. I think to satisfy the demands of my heart for joy and … still, you know, there's something wild in me that makes me also destroy love. But each time when I wake up and realize that those early sensations of rapture have vanished, I know that I must begin again … over and over and over."

"Your situation is curious, you know that, eh? Or is that an English outlook? So, what are you looking for? Perfection? Did none of the women of your life measure up?"

"Manfred, you're married, have children, you've found yourself. I think I'm always looking for something that might be different. I've long thought I'm searching for the source."

"The source?"

"The root of everything. The source of all things. Like the most satisfying part of my studies in linguistics in England was the search for the Indo-European roots of words."

Karl had lovingly christened his lady friends with nicknames reflecting their characters or the characteristics he would have wanted in them. Peculiar source names like "Waterdrop" or "Trickle" or "Spring" or "Root". He still thought of Janet, the London girl he'd loved the longest, as "Fountainhead". At the time he'd been writing his dissertation on the relationship between the origins of the Danube River, the *Donau,* and the diverse languages spoken along its route to the sea. His work was based on a *Wandersommer* with schoolmates from England, hiking through the mountains and hills and vales of southwestern Germany searching for the source of the Danube. He perceived an enormous satisfaction when he found it and tasted the first drops of water bubbling and trickling from the earth at the great river's source. Therefore subsequent cruises along the blue Danube from Vienna were each time major life events. He loved elaborating on his visits over the Danube's 2,850-kilometer length through Austria, Slovakia, Hungary, Croatia, Serbia, Romania, Bulgaria, Moldova, and Ukraine to its mouth where it drains into the Black Sea.

"Consequently, I came to understand that deep sea between Europe and Asia in the same way I did the female sex. The ancient sea was deep, dark and mysterious and concealed old secrets: disturbingly magical, the Sea's waters flow in two directions, a surface current carrying the Black Sea's cold waters southwards into the Aegean Sea of the Greeks and an undercurrent from the warmer Aegean flowing in the opposite direction. Must be why the Black Sea terrified Persian and Greek sailors of yore."

Terrifying and unnatural to others, but not to Karl who had long experienced his mind as the battleground between his lower current conscience and his high current self-esteem.

2.

Although Karl Rasch was eternally on the qui vive for love, since he began teaching in the Gymnasium he had followed strictly one rule of exclusivity: no romantic involvement with any of the nineteen-year-old beauties in his class who flirted outrageously with him. Never! In fact, his abrupt departure from England after his years of school and university was caused by the definitive break-up with that Italian graduate student at Essex where he read history. And he knew that in his manner he had loved in a special way his Alessandra, who in that terrible "romantic" way put a final end to their relationship and to his life in England.

Earlier in his life, Karl had become convinced that ordinary passion was only an idea. If, on the other hand, passion was genuine it would last a lifetime, though in forms not usually associated with the first rapture of love. It might begin simply as the uncontrolled explosion of the youthful heart, a heart perhaps not even ready for romantic love. Ordinary love passion was like that quiet source of the Danube in southern Germany, like those first bubbles quickly becoming drops, joining together in rivulets, merging then into a gentle stream becoming love which, near Ingolstadt, transforms into a river and takes the name, the *Donau. Die schöne blaue Donau.* The Danube meets other rivers and grows and matures and ages on its way to the Black Sea. His imaginary utopian love was like that river he had followed for so long. He understood. A beautiful image indeed. But he had remained immune to the lures of "falling in love".

The pure passion of what is called 'falling in love'—a theoretical step that Karl had avoided like a microbe in the times of the plague—begins noisily like a great waterfall fully aware that it is a great waterfall, only to slow gradually and, if it is what it seems, it finds its real path as its waters become great rivers. Water goes where it wants to go. The passion he had in mind had the power to cement a relationship of love.

"Body and soul," he began his eleven o'clock lesson one morning. From the moment he'd taken his place before the class that day, distracted by Gloria's exposed thighs and her amber wolfish eyes fixed in his, he was already regretting he'd chosen the body subject for these sex-driven maidens. Her incessant shifting around in her chair just in front of him and her sensually crossing and uncrossing her beautiful tanned legs added to his befuddlement.

"Uh, yes ... so goes the love song. To love, uh, body and soul. Well, we know what the body is and we" ....

Karl paused, pretending to check his notes once more but in reality flustered by Gloria's drawn-out un-crossing of one leg and then lifting unnecessarily high the other in her constant adjusting of her position. Was her smile not unusually mocking today? Was she not deriding his inability to control his embarrassment? In any case, Karl was uncertain as to how to handle this authentic Teutonic Messalina.

"But again and again we ask what is the body, er, no, no, that is to say, what is the soul?" Someone suppressed a giggle. Gloria laughed out loud. And the only two boys in the class nudged each other and smirked.

"Nobody knows," Karl managed to continue, raising one hand to shush the girls and again wishing he'd never gotten into the body business. Dangerous topic in this room pervaded by female scents drifting erotically through the still air before swirling around the susceptible head of Professor Rasch.

"But if the soul does exist, which comes first? Body or soul? Which depends on which? Maybe they are independent one of the other ... if the soul even exists, that is. In any case, this philosophical soul hypothesis enhances and elevates the role of the mind also. For as they thought in the times of Socrates the mind counts. Yet, among the philosopher's followers, the human's capacity of recollection assumed the existence of the soul which, though not necessarily immortal, is an invisible force that animates us. Thus the soul is associated with memories, passions and values, things that each of us cares about. In any case, Socrates ultimately discarded the idea of the existence of a soul ... he concluded that we don't need one since we have the brain that controls all. However, Plato, the great soul speculator then postulated that we do not really learn new things at all; we simply recall things we knew before birth. And that transmission, he surmised, is the role of the soul and perhaps also the mind. Even though they have no mass, no space nor location, the mind, and the soul do regulate the … er, the body. And, Ladies and Gentlemen, the body is something real."

He paused and looked over the class as if expecting their cynical applause. That word, body, still hung over him and the girls like a neon sign. He had gotten into the body thing, and somehow, he had to finish this lecture once and for all. Hopefully on a high point and not a gaffe.

"One and a half millennia later Descartes differentiated between soul and mind. For him, the mind was linked closely to the body. Like the body the mind was mortal and divided into different parts, he thought; the soul on the other hand was eternal and indivisible. Then for two hundred years Descartes' eternal soul hypothesis faded, almost forgotten. But today in our times a swerve has occurred: the soul is again fashionable. A philosophical splurge is underway. The soul marks every good poem we read, every song we hear, every work of art that holds us. Read your Wordsworth. That sudden Wordsworthian revelation arrives like an epiphany and you perceive the click of harmony between you and the world. The soul has revealed itself to you.

"Today we talk and speculate about the soul. Yet, at the same time, we accept—albeit many people reluctantly—that the brain performs all the functions attributed to the soul: mental activity, perception of sensations, storage for memories like the memory of what we have been, reasoning about the soul itself, and decision-making about how to deal with life. But the reality is that noneof these, not the soul, mind, or brain, are for the human being a satisfying substitute for the body … without which all the rest is just intellectual, religious masturbation."

In that moment he heard as if from afar, apart from form and body, like a breath, the enchanting melodious voice of Gloria-Messalina sing: "Amen."

"Now, friends and fellow learners, make your choices. *Les jeux sont faits, rien ne va plus.*"

On the spot, he chose to raise the white flag and abandon the Gymnasium ship. The subject was too difficult to discuss with a room full of tantalizing females. A bell echoed somewhere in the distance. He appeared deep in soulful thought. Unhurriedly, the girls made their way out, looking over their shoulders at glorious Gloria who remained seated, her knees now pressed primly together. They stared at each other. She blushing in victory, he confused in retreat. She smiled her challenging smile. Karl was undecided: tear up his notes ostentatiously in front of her or file them away with the others. He cleared his throat, smiled professorially, folded the notes into a precise square, and stuffed them into his back pocket.

"*Auf Wiedersehen*, Gloria," he said and left the room somewhat piously. He had just laid out for Gloria his rule: no fucking around with women under twenty.

However, in the preparation of the body lesson, Karl had forgotten that Catholic Bavaria was still what it had always been: super Catholic and bigoted up to the priests' ears. Someone in his class, likely one of the two jealous males, he suspected, went to the powerful *Studienrat* and reported his unabashed sexual allusions made to the cream of Bavarian Catholic womanhood. Consequently, Karl was summoned to appear before the dreaded Study Council at ten a.m. the following morning. When Karl entered the conference room and saw the four women and one man of the Council on one side of the notorious long oak table, he breathed a sigh of relief: he knew his academic survival had greater chances before a group of mature women. He greeted them and smiled modestly as he took the chair opposite them. After the Committee Chairwoman stated the reasons for the summons—Karl's certain unspecified allusions to a class of honorable young ladies, the cream of Munich society—the Council felt obligated to hear professor Rasch's version of events before reaching a decision on the proper action to take.

Karl cleared his throat, crossed one leg over the other reminding himself—*verdamnt noch mal*—of Gloria, and began rather pompously the prepared spiel he was certain the ladies wanted to hear: "Ladies and Gentleman, I want to assure you that the lodestar, the very guiding principle in my lectures to these young people preparing to step into the world, has always been—and always will be—my firm endeavor to propose thoughts and ideas for them to resolve in their own search for truth. The mystery of the soul in the human being is currently the subject of wide debate and discussion in intellectual circles which these graduating young people will soon experience. Now, as religious people understand, any discussion of the soul concerns first of all its very existence. What is the soul? Where is it? What is its role? Such discussion invariably involves the mind, the brain, and last but not least the body which hosts them. That in short was the subject of my eleven a.m. lecture yesterday, the notes for which are in my files and available to any and all."

The ladies, not surprisingly easily and quickly convinced by a few well-selected intellectual-ringing words—and coming from their handsome Humanities Professor—looked one to the other, nodding in obvious agreement with Karl's words. "Oh, I don't think any action of our part will be necessary Professor Rasch. You have clarified the situation as reported to us to our satisfaction." It had taken less than four minutes. The formality was thus accomplished; they could now assure parents that their children were in the best of hands, so to speak. After a brief deliberation, the Gymnasium Council decided the informal hearing sufficient to muzzle any charges that the Gymnasium was dithering in the world of sex masked as Humanities.

When the closure bell sounded the day after the *Studienrat* hearing Karl asked the two male students in his class to remain for a moment. They shrugged carelessly and came forward just as matter-of-factly. "Yes, Professor Rasch."

"Let's see, you are Heinrich and Hartmund," Karl said checking the list of fifteen names. "So, who's who?" "I'm Heinrich," said one. "So I'm Hartmund," said the other.

"Okay, listen, guys, I got into a bit of trouble about that lesson ... you know which lesson I mean. I want to know one thing. Did you guys report it as improper?"

"Honest to God, we didn't squeal on you," Heinrich or Hartmund said, hand over heart. "But we suspect one of the girls did," the other said.

"Which girl, Heinrich?"

"I'm Hartmund and I suspect the one who stayed behind after the others left the room, the one who..."

"Whoa there, Heinrich-Hartmund, I just told Gloria she had to understand that I don't f…, uh, that I don't play around with teenagers … and good-bye."

3.

For over a week after the body incident, Karl was downcast. He felt a void inside him. His eyes were dull, his movements laggard. Yet, inside, he was not the calm person his friends knew. Though externally sad, his inner tension was stretched to the snapping point. And he knew why. For the first time in his memory, there was no woman in his life. No woman to love and to love him. He felt turned inside out, eviscerated, his heart ripped from his breast. When would he meet the woman of his life? Most certainly not in the city's Beer Gardens. Nor among his students. So afternoons he began walking the city streets, through the winding backstreets in the Old Town, he hung around fashion boutiques in the shopping passages, he sat in cafés and frequented public places. In the theater, he lingered in the lobbies at intermission. He was eternally waiting, waiting for her to appear. He sensed he would soon meet the woman who would change his life.

Late one Saturday morning he was in the Lenbachhaus Art Museum to see the Blue Rider painters … good and safe lecture material. For some reason he had awakened early that morning recalling vaguely a dream image of himself just before waking and his saying in English—his most frequent dream language—to an unknown woman that today he felt he was a different kind of German. His oneiric words reflected his conscious view of himself: he felt like an internal migrant. Not English, but also a stranger in his homeland. Going from one gallery to the next in the Lenbachhaus he still felt the dream alive in him; he knew the sensation would remain with him all day, on the surface of his consciousness.

He was examining Jawlensky's *The Hunchback* and trying to understand why a figure like the handsome young man of the picture—whose disfigurement was not visible—should mean bad luck for anyone meeting him. At the same time, out of the corner of his eye, he noted the same woman he'd seen near him earlier observing works by Kandinsky.

"I don't understand," he said rather loudly in English to no one in particular.

"I don't either," said the woman, despite the usual museum *shhh's* sounding from other parts of the gallery.

Karl turned to her. She looked familiar, like someone from an earlier life. Maybe a girl in the English school when he'd lived with his parents in Surrey. Or like one of those faces out of a half forgotten dream. Or was she the very same woman from this morning's dream? He liked to imagine such paranormal events that he never related to anyone else. "Haven't we met before?" he asked her in reference to the dream woman and wishing he'd retained a clearer image of her physical appearance. Oh, if she were only the same! he thought, remembering the time he was driving through the countryside on his way back from Manchester and saw a barely moving object in a sunny afternoon sky. But only the next day back at home the object's image passed from his brain or mind or soul to his eyes: he had seen a UFO, huge, round, dark and frightening, just as it was supposed to be.

"I don't know ... I don't think so," she said with all the naturalness in the world. "What do you think?" she added with a slight smile.

Karl peered at her closely, the dream woman in his mind. "In German fairy tales, hunchbacks bring bad luck," he said. "Like a broken mirror or a black cat."

"We have the same bad luck objects in Sweden." She spoke with his same English accent and had deep, passionate—something between wild and demonic—surprisingly light blue eyes like his. Karl stared hard into those eyes as if remembering something of the distant past. He thought: 'Her very soul is in those eyes.' If Alessandra had once had a soul in her eyes, her tears had washed it away so that at the end she had none whatsoever. She needed it back, but her soul was gone, never to return. Alessandra? Karl held his many doubts secret: had he stolen and destroyed her very soul? Now however, there was only the fading memory of what they had been together.

On the spur of the moment and still a little dream drunk. Karl stepped closer to the woman, clamped his hands on her arms, leaned forward and kissed her on the lips. He was most surprised when she kissed him back.

He leaned backwards, his body still pressed against hers, and said: "I'm Karl Maria Rasch. According to my dream self I'm a new kind of German and you, you're a new kind of love. You see, we already met … in my last night's dream ... or perhaps long ago." He looked down left and right at her arms over his shoulders. She was looking him straight in the eyes. Both ignored the shhhsing people in their gallery even though they were nearly whispering from sudden emotion.

"My name is Harriet."

"Harriet! How wonderful! Harriet! I love that name but I've never known one before. Never known a Harriet. Oh, at last. You'll be Harriet forever."

"And I've never known a man called Maria before … I might call you Maria just for the hell of it."

"My father loved a poet named Rainer Maria Rilke who was only called Rilke … too great a poet to be called Maria. Harriet! Harriet what?"

"Stendahl. Harriet Stendahl. My father claimed he was a very distant relative of the other Stendahl. Who knows?"

"Harriet, now that we've kissed, let's blow this place … uh, this beloved place." Turning back to Jawlensky, he said "Sorry for that slip, Alexej. This beautiful woman's fault."

Harriet was average height, short raven black hair, big unshadowed eyes, no make-up at all, shapely body down-played by a simple light blue blouse, a knee-length brown skirt, and a somewhat matching cardigan. She dressed like Karl, careless but tasteful … except for her breath-robbing red pumps highlighting perfect Swedish legs. Harriet was beautiful. The most beautiful woman he'd ever seen, the most beautiful woman he'd ever loved. They looked at each other in silence. Both felt an awkward timidity in their hands that found no definite place. Hesitation and indecision in their eyes … less it seemed in her soul-filled eyes in which Karl noted also a certain impishness. Yet, yet, there in the Blue Rider Gallery in the Lenbachhaus Museum still in front of *The Hunchback*, a secret, ancient but enduring signal passed between them. Karl felt they had known each other before they were born. They both understood the message. Only chosen souls, he thought, have the gift of understanding that they are the children of a secret Destiny. Karl saw his fate and she hers in the eyes of the other. That secret attraction arriving from existence hypnotized both Karl and Harriet. Only superficial paltry persons would not see their Destiny standing before them. To be blind to love, Karl thought, would be to accept that the soul is just thrown into humans to amuse their creators and in order to make them suffer.

Wordlessly they left the museum together. Words, Karl felt, would spoil the enchantment. The bright sun was switched on dim mode; the city lay in a mist; the entire solar brilliance of the morning had settled inside them. Luisenstrasse was all the streets of Munich. Harriet took his hand.

"I don't know how I dared kiss you," he finally said as they stepped onto the green park-like square where Nazis had once built party buildings and paved it with granite stones as a parade ground for their torch-lit ceremonies. Karl was more modest and old-fashioned than he'd imagined himself.

"I know how I dared kiss you back," Harriet said, pressing her coal-black hair against his arm. "I recognized you … and I now know myself better."

"Why, what are you … besides a beautiful Swede … and you know yourself?""I was just starting a job in the planetarium when a friend at the city newspaper of Malmo asked if I wanted to come here as a correspondent … low pay but good experience. So now I'm in München with you in my arms. That's experience. But it's maybe also Destiny."

"I have a feeling you've got lots of that, experience, I mean. From the way you kissed me. But destiny? I was just thinking about the same. What if one of us hadn't gone to the museum today?"

"Kissed you back, you mean. You started it. Oh, I have some! I do know men. I've loved some of them and have been loved, too. Maybe I'll share things with you. Anyway, we would've met somewhere else. Or at another time."

"You remind me of me. Crazy, you know! And that we met … like that."

"You never know in life, do you? Say, where're we going?"

"Just walking. You want some lunch? I know a place. A café-restaurant. And next door the hotel I lived in for several months when I returned from merry England. Nostalgic kind of place. Lots of fond memories."

"Hotel, eh? Okay, let's go there."

"Restaurant or hotel?"

"Oh, you choose. But I am hungry ... I'm always hungry. My hungry nature."

Arm in arm, an occasional kiss, they arrived at a wide avenue, a major artery reaching straight northwards toward Schwabing and outside the city to Dachau. He wondered if that name was still embarrassing to real Germans. It was to him. They stood at the stoplight looking left and right. Harriet's hand tightened in his. He kept pressing the button for the pedestrian green light. Some people had made it to the pedestrian island in the middle of the avenue. People shouted to each other across the wide street. Come on, *los*, *los*! Clanging trams passed in both directions. Buses and trucks, plus the usual Saturday midday traffic created a mobile metal inferno. Harriet took his arm in both her hands.

"No, no," she said. "Not to that place out in the middle." He looked down at her pressing against him, saw the panic on her face. "Okay, Harriet, we'll hurry across. Don't worry. We'll leave the moment the light changes. Like two Galapagos turtles we'll make to the other side."

Gisela's Café was packed. Saturday noontime crowd. They got a table in the side garden. Vine-covered. Red grapes dangling. Karl saw them immediately. Only a few tables away Gloria-Messalina reigned like a queen over her circle.

"Hey, Prof, body or soul today?" Gloria said passing nearby, a skirt about twelve inches above her knees and a dangerously low-cut décolleté. Half naked, Karl thought. Over her shoulder, she waved at her friends.

Karl frowned.

"Now who was that?" a revived Harriet asked sardonically. "Body and soul?" "They're all in my Humanities class. She's been trying to, well, I don't know what, maybe seduce me."

"Probably not hard to do." Harriet grinned evilly. "As they say in an expression we learned at my English school, eventually the birds come home to roost."

"Harriet. I got into trouble over a lecture about the soul … and the body. The *Studienrat* summoned me for a hearing. Too much emphasis on the body for those proper girls. I convinced the council the soul was widely discussed in intellectual circles. Somebody'd reported me, maybe that girl herself … or those two boys over at the table … Heinrich and Hartmund. Could never tell them apart. They both love sexy Gloria. Jealous types."

"Hmm! We Swedes don't think much about the soul. But Descartes who died in Stockholm thought a lot about the dualism of mind and body … mind or soul about the same thing for him. You know, his Cogito ergo sum. Anyway I couldn't digest his treatise *Passions of the Soul.* Not even interested. He was your exact opposite, too much soul and too little body."

"Okay, Harriet. But speaking of the body I have to ask about your fear when we crossed Leopoldstrasse. It was more than caution. It was panic. What's that all about?"

"I was twelve and empty-headed. One day after school a yellow government bus hit me on a busy street. Lots of operations to put me back together again. I still get anxiety attacks … in street traffic like that. Psychiatrists eliminated the panic attacks that immobilized me. But panic comes back at times … like crossing that street. But look here, Karl, are we going to sit here and watch that sexy student of yours and talk about panic or are we going to drink some beer and maybe go to that hotel."

"Harriet! Oh, how I … how I love to say that name."

"Is that what you really meant to say?"

"Oh, I was thinking about the drinks, too. Don't you want some wine instead? We can try their Valpolicella. From North Italy That's the red wine everybody in this city drinks. Let's have some."

"Okay. But I want the beer, too."

"Ah, you Swedes. Okay, we'll have both. We used to drink it like that in merry England … and with a shot of whiskey upfront. We called it the Bloody Triangle.""Marianne," Karl said to the waitress nearby, "please give us a Bloody Triangle."

"Both of you?"

"Both of us … one each … for now."

After the first round of that magic drink, Harriet said. "Ah, now life's worth living. So let's get serious. What did you intend to say before? Just say it and get it over with. And let's have another Bloody Mary."

"Triangle, Harriet. Bloody Triangle. What in the world did you study those years at the university, alcohol, its properties and effects?"

"If you absolutely have to know I got my Ph.D. in astrophysics at Cambridge."

"For Christsakes, why didn't you say so?"

"Say so? When?"

"Oh, I don't know … at some point."

"I'm risking saying it now."

"Risking? Why risking?"

"Astrophysics frightens men."

"Well, what was your specialization in that frightening field?"

"Extrasolar planets and their emissions across the electromagnetic spectrum. Their properties like luminosity, density, temperature, and chemical composition. Of course, all that involves a lot of theoretical work and observational physics."

"Oh, Harriet, is that all astrophysics is? Doesn't scare fearless me in the least."

"Then I can tell you the rest and be done with it. I'm most fascinated by attempts to determine the properties of dark matter, dark energy, black holes, and whether time travel is possible and if the multiverse even exists. You can get a Nobel for that stuff! What we really want to know is the origin and ultimate fate of the universe. And Karl, I also climb buildings."

"Climb buildings? What does that mean? And where? What buildings?"

"I'm President of Free Climbers of East Malmo. Always trying to reach the stars! But I do mostly Buildering … building climbing. Started it at Cambridge. It's illegal in Malmo ... so I have a police record."

"Harriet, you're a criminal then. Your words touch me. They're scary. Terrifying for a pure earthling, body-oriented man like me. I've never thought of free climbing but I would like to know about time travel. Does that make me an aspirant astrophysicist?"

"To answer you, I have to ask you a question first?"

"Shoot!"

"Do you ever have the haunting feeling that time is running out? I mean, all time is just ... just running out."

"I have that feeling all the time. That's my ultimate message to my class. Time is running out. But I haven't said it yet. If the school board was upset because I talked allusively about the body, what would they say if I taught the girls that time was running out?"

"Nothing! They would say nothing. You can't talk about the sexual component of human life because the good hypocritical bourgeois society suppresses that form of humanness. Suppresses the most human part. They think it is a stain and must be concealed. But they have no idea about dark energy and black holes. And time running out rings romantic to them, like a Graham Greene novel."

"So I qualify as an astrophysicist?"

"Sort of ... so tell me your secret! Now!"

"It's simpler than the search for the multiverse but tremendous at the same time. In this moment I'm doing what I was always afraid of, Harriet. Harriet, I'm falling in love. I always heard it came like this, like a bolt out of the blue of the universe. Extremely dangerous. One of the risky acts of your life. And also decisive. And I'm afraid it can only happen once to me. I've loved many times but I've never fallen in love. I don't know exactly what that is but it's different from just loving. The difference is indefinable. You fall in love and then, maybe, little by little, you learn to really love ... uh, body and soul. You see, I speculate, too."

He studied Harriet looking him straight in the eyes as was her way. He drank off another Dornkaat that had appeared on its own ... as if out of a black hole, he thought.

"I've always been looking for the source of things. I loved Alessandra in England but then she fell in love ... with me. And she killed herself near Oxford. That's why I'm here now ... and falling in love with a hard-drinking Swedish astrophysicist who's gazing toward the multiverse but is afraid of crossing broad avenues."

"So that's it," Harriet muttered, her expression suddenly grim. "Some things can be fixed, some things ...."

"Don't say it, Harriet. Just wait a second, gotta see Gisela. Drink your Mary and I'll be right back." Her shot glass was empty when Karl came back. They clinked beer glasses and Karl opened his left hand on the table and pushed a red key card toward Harriet. She stared at it for long seconds, picked it up, and examined it suspiciously as if it were a trap. Abruptly she stood up, her impish grin back and said:

"Let's go, Lover!"

Karl hesitated, somewhat offended, and thinking, thinking, thinking. The Old Karl would have spoken her words first. After all, he brought the red key card. Now he played the dummy. Let her lead the way. Did that make it all right even if he was falling in love? Was it all the same? Or was falling in love just bullshit? Like time travel bullshit. The multiverse. The audacity of these astrophysicists!

4.

Karl felt new in the world, like an explorer arriving in a new land. He felt like he used to on his arrival in each new love. But more so. More powerful. He felt emboldened by the newness of his 'falling in love'. He was no longer compelled to think in ordinary terms about this new self. Unlike his old self back in the times when he thought in simplified binary terms of male and female, true and false, faithful and unfaithful, loyal and treacherous. Now that he had 'fallen in love', Harriet became primary. He had transcended his old monotonous self. His transcendence projected a new dimension of his existence beyond mediocre considerations of the quality of the male-female relationship. With each of her breaths as she slept during the early morning hours, he had perceived a sense of a restorative peace come over him which he had never experienced when he was the loved one, when he was the

Benjamin in the multicolored coat. In his nocturnal perceptions of his pre-Harriet being, he saw his love for one or the other of his former loves as mere repetition. This morning up here in Paradise, he roamed far and wide and endlessly free in the new territories of his sense of perception of himself. What would the Gymnasium be without "the Humanities" class? What would humanity itself be without love? Doesn't love, this all-powerful sympathy for another person, this linking of two souls, can this same eternal love not exist also between peoples? His only answer was Harriet and himself. When Harriet awoke basking under the sunshine beaming through the skylight he told her about Paradise. From the top floor of Gisela's Hotel, he pointed out the views through the uncovered skylight and the wide windows looking out over the dark green carpet of the wooded corner of the English Garden. To the left, the green steeple of the Chinese Tower and to the right the twin pillars of the Frauenkirche, the view which had prompted the name Paradise he had once bestowed on this his temporary home. Harriet would always use the Swedish, *Paradis*.

"What would you like to do today, Harriet?"

"Do we have to leave Paradis?"

"We don't have to but we can choose … a rare gift these days. A privilege really. We can go back to the café next door … or stay up here in Paradise. Harriet, do you love me?"

"I don't want to choose. Yes, I love you. I want to go beer drinking but I'm afraid if we go down to the ground we can lose Paradis."

"Look, you see that tower over there above the treetops? We can go beer drinking there, hardly losing sight of Paradise. When we get tired of beer drinking we can return … for all today and tomorrow too we will hold onto Paradise. It's ours for the holding. Harriet, are you in love with me?"

"Can we have breakfast, too? You know I'm always hungry. And yes, I think I'm falling in love with you, with us, with Paradis. All today. Every day. We'll live always in today."

"Yes, we'll live in today. Harriet, do you dream?"

"I just dreamed of a dream in which you are saying we will never cry because tears are for the past. We are the present and the future, you're saying in the dream I'm dreaming. We've abandoned the past."

"What I want to know is if in that dream you're dreaming you're falling in love with me."

"Falling, falling, falling. I'm there. I've arrived. I've fallen in love."

"One thing though, Harriet. That abandon the past thing was just a bad dream. Who wants to forget the past? Sometimes we say we want to forget the past. But we don't … not really. Last night together, just hours ago, minutes ago, is the past. But it's part of the present. Our new present, uh, a present enriched by that past. And it will get richer and richer. A person without the past is dead. The same for a whole people. A whole nation. No, Harriet, we don't want to forget the past. We can't even do without the pain of the past. It's yours, only yours. Oh, most of us could have done things differently, Harriet. The past is present. Done and finished, yes, but it's still part of the present. It's fixed. You can trust it. It will remain the same … except for the time of your stars and interstellar bodies. Are they past or future? Maybe their past is all time, always, past-present-future. All one, if, as T.S. Eliot writes, *all time is eternally present*. Oh, I don't know what I'm saying or how I got onto this subject but anyway we humans can't change the past. Time travel is intriguing but it would turn everything upside down. Go back and do it again? Better … or worse? No, we can't live it again but we don't forget the past. Not all of it. It's everything, Harriet. It's our life. Without it, we're nothing. It may hide behind a veil of oblivion, but as Freud says, it's always there. It's your shadow you, always present. If it's not in your conscious, it lies deeper, now quietly, now rowdily, but there. Something always remains. Maybe residing in a corner of your subconscious, elusive and slippery, or wandering around lost and unwanted. But it's there, illuminating and nourishing some … and killing others. For the past is also murderous. Slowly, ever so slowly, it kills. Like my love killed Alessandra. So did I kill Alessandra? Remembrances have the capacity to soothe you and pave the way for your acceptance of what really happened … or it can destroy you. We don't want to admit it, Harriet, but the real mystery is the future we're waiting for. And you're the source of our future. It has to begin somewhere! So it springs from you."

5.

It might have been Harriet's purposeful approach toward the row of tables near the pagoda-like five-tiered *Chinesischer Turm* that convinced two Lederhosen-clad oldsters from Upper Bavaria to rise unsteadily, slap down drunkenly a lavish tip and liberate a choice table near a small stream and a row of chestnut trees.

"This is a sacred hour for the consumption of Hofbräu beer. God knows of what alcoholic kick today. In any case, this beer is brewed for a special effect on Saturday mornings in October … and for us. Now just a moment of patience! Self-service here." Karl returned with two huge Mass' of Hofbräu beer and a bag of pretzels tucked under his arm: "Harriet, I once saw a waitress at the Oktoberfest carry ten of these one-liter mugs at once. Now off we go! Beer drinking. This is strong stuff. If it doesn't make you drunk within the hour, nothing will."

"Hey, where's the Dornkaat?" she countered suspiciously as if he were holding something back from her.

A slight breeze blew, the chestnuts rustled, the stream trickled, white harmless clouds floated past, tourists swarmed, and stopped in front of the pagoda tower to make selfies. Harriet and Karl drank, they kissed, they drank another round, then another.

"Harriet, your beautiful blue eyes are zonking. See, I told you so, Harriet, I told you so. You're nearly ripe drunk."

"Whassh that, whassh that, rip drunk?"

"Not rip drunk. Zonking eyes, ripe drunk."

"Okay, shoo what? Lessh' go back to Paradissh then."

"But I wanted to talk about morality with an astrophysicist."

"Later, later, lessh go back to Paradissh. Oh, I'm a little sick."

"Ashtrophysicccisst can't drink Oktoberfest beer."

"Lessh ride a horshe back to Paradissh. Oh, I'm going to vomit."

So while Harriet threw up in the creek, drunken Karl fetched a huge jar of black coffee and aspirin. "Ah, those Bavarian Chinese, always well-prepared."

They drank coffee and ate pretzels until their eyes unzonked. Harriet said to cancel the horse and have lunch. With the tip the Bavarians had left they got a table on the third level of the tower and gradually returned to real life.

Riding back through the park in a horse-drawn carriage, Harriet threw her head back onto a cushion and took several seconds long gulps of what she decided was pine-flavored air. Karl kept kissing her and repeating he couldn't wait to get back to Paradise.

"Paradis, Paradis, where art thou? Words of someone important. Milton? Or is it lost, Karl? Did Milton say it? Did he mean that Paradis can get lost like the biblical one? Yes, maybe Milton. Too bad you didn't vomit too, Karl. We could have done it together."

"Romantic idea! Now that's falling in love, Harriet! You can't even throw up without me. How did we miss each other until now? Yes, Milton, I'm pretty sure."

That night at eleven Harriet was hungry. So again they descended from Paradise. Karl assured Harriet it would wait for them. The lovers would return. When they re-crossed the wide avenue, love-drunk Harriet didn't blink. A small all-night restaurant in the Schelling Strasse. They had *Kalbsbraten mit Semmelknödeln.* Harriet ate half of his. They had Apfelstrudel. Harriet ate half of his. They returned to the Valpolicella. Again Karl said that everybody in Munich was drinking the same red wine … from North Italy, he added.

"Compared to the Hofbräu beer and Dornkaat it goes down like freshwater," Harriet said.

"Where the hell did you learn to drink like you do? Were you a sailor? Or did you work in some drink-infested tropical jungle?"

"Swedes love alcohol. But because of alcohol control laws, people take the ferry over to Finland to drink all they want. Everybody in my home in Malmo drank like fish. We're rich and our house is big. You might not believe it but we had five bars in the house. My father had his private cognac bar, hidden in one place or another; my mother had her secret bar with her favorites; my sister, hers. So I had one too. Then there was the official bar for guests. We drank all the time. Someone of us was always drunk. I had to leave home in order to stay sober enough to study. The time I got run over by the yellow bus, my father came to the hospital stinking fish drinking drunk. Crazy home, mine."

"Mine was a teetotaler society in comparison. We only drank beer and cocktails if my parents threw a party. I learned on my own. Speaking of drinking habits ...."

Karl ordered a second bottle. Thinking of their meeting in the Lenbachhaus he asked Harriet if she believed in Destiny. She took a long drink of Valpolicella and said: "I don't know for sure but I believe Fate plays a bigger role in our lives. Like my being run over by a government bus. A yellow bus changed my life and maybe made me look for the stars and become an astrophysicist. But actually, Fate seems to be most often bad Fate. So maybe good things can be Destiny."

"That's interesting because though the terms are used interchangeably some philosophers believe that our future is the will of one intelligent force or that it is simply the predetermined outcome of the laws of nature. Others think Fate is the same as Destiny, just stronger. Still others, like myself, think such matters are determined by pure chance ... like our meeting in the Lenbachhaus. Now I'm changing horses. I'm falling for Destiny, too."

"I think it was our Destiny to meet ... but not necessarily there."

"Yes, yes, it was. Still, Chance had us both in the same place at the same time. That's why the God Chance has been defined as the unpredictable spontaneity of the atoms in their course, somehow linked to DNA and genetics."

"Pretty weak theory. No, absolutely not. No astrophysicist could seriously go along with that."

"Well, listen. I read of a wild theory that Destiny may be hereditary. Try to get a handle on that, Harriet! Some theory-crazed scientists decided that our defects are written in our genes. And that ipso facto the deciphered genome can reveal our fate. Fate, a matter of genetics, Harriet! That by deconstructing and stitching together the DNA's molecules, genetic engineering and molecular biology can rebuild them as a new genome, a new destiny ... or a new something."

"Then I'll stay with the stars ...and falling in love."

It was two a.m. The lovers stood with heads turned upwards toward the stars. They'd forgotten the red key card. Lunar beams turned their faces deathly white. The Bloody Triangle café was closed tight. Moon rays skipped along the sides of the Gisela Hotel, spotlighting the fifth-floor balcony of Paradise. They were both cold stone sober again. Harriet pawed the sidewalk in disillusionment.

"How could we've been so stupid? Now, what can we do? Just wait here till dawn?"

"Harriet, Harriet! It's not a tragedy. My apartment is not far away. We can go there … if we want." Karl's voice was marked by a sudden perceptible sense of humiliation. The falling in love, he was thinking, is not yet complete.

"That's not the point. We have the right to our second night right here. In Paradis. It was decided. There has to be a way.… Hey, Karl, wait a minute. I was forgetting my free climbing skills. All I have to do is scale this wall to the balcony where the door to Paradis is open. See that drainpipe? It's a walkway to the stars. A three-minute climb at the most. I'll drop the key card down to you."

"You're nuts," Karl said, tapping and pulling at the rusty drainpipe. "This wouldn't support the weight of a squirrel. No, Harriet, no free climbing here." "You'll see in a moment," Harriet said, kicking off her red pumps while her sensitive fingers found invisible holds, one hand on the drainpipe, the fingers of her other hand bent into another hidden crevice.

"Nothing stops a Builder free climber."

Before Karl could stop her she was off like a shot toward the stars. She paused between the second and third floors. A stray night cloud passed. Harriet shouted something about the moon rays. Then again she was off full speed upwards.

Moonbeams illuminated Harriet's bare legs and her right shoulder and the side of her face looking toward the stars. Her right arm was frozen in the act of reaching toward the balcony lit up like a theater stage. "Karl," she shouted, "you should be up here the moon rays are absolutely …"

In that instant, he heard a crack like lightning striking a bundle of telephone wires. Frozen in horror he watched the drainpipe in which her left foot was embedded literally fly apart, twisting and writhing as it detached itself from the wall and from Harriet's foot.

"Karl I …"

And she, too, slowly, slowly began slipping and sliding and grappling with air as her body began to fall. Silence reigned. Eternal. Everything happened in slow motion as Harriet dropped downwards, fourth floor, third, now sailing as she passed the second floor, the first, and in the same instant smashed full force into the confused oblivion of her body's merging and melding into Karl.

Coyoacán - Place of Coyotes

(Lost Importance)

Broken spears lie in the roads;
We have torn our hair in grief
The houses are roofless now, and their walls
are red with blood.
(An Aztec poem about the fall of an empire)

1.

Ethan was sitting at the sidewalk café on the main plaza of Coyoacán mulling over the implications of his unspoken declaration of independence from his wife, Guadalupe. The other tables were vacant as often in the early afternoon. The daily tropical shower had come and gone. And shining through a veil of mist the September sun had turned the trees in the park vis-à-vis to silver. Something about being alone in the café reminded him of his youth when he would stand on the city square at the top of the hill under the shadow of Sunset Mountain and the same feeling of lostness came over him. In the hope of discovering his original self in his first home of so long ago, he let the remembrance carry him back; instead, the conceptual return to that past soured and turned into sadness; he felt he was now only a blurred ghost on the fugitive square under the green mountain. Ethan disliked parting with the past.

Coyoacán. At over two thousand meters altitude the temperature was perfect. and he perceived acutely the sensation of being at the top of the world. As each time that feeling arrived he inhaled deeply and the air seemed the essence of purity though he knew the toxic air infecting this city dominated even fleeting illusions of purity.

He squinted in the direction of where Popocatepetl and Iztaccihuatl were supposed to be, scanning the horizon in the hope that the curtain of invisible pollution had magically lifted and revealed the magnificence of the two volcanoes. But not even the vaguest outline of a mountain was visible. Man-made impurity was greater than nature itself. And again his insistent memory rebounded to the air of an ephemeral world apart from Mexico City, a world in the Blue Ridge Mountains where Mount Mitchel was majestically present, a vision which brought back from his deepest conscious his father's simple feelings about nature: to him the mountainous curtain hanging between him and the flat country where he'd grown up was an obstacle to be overcome, not a magical geological giant. And so he too, the young Ethan, began to see the mountains as a wall separating him from the real world beyond. But after he broke through nature's barricade and saw what lay in the beyond, he missed the mountains, which now, once more, played a major role in his life. Oh, if he could only see 'Popo'. The real top of the world where all things would become clear. The great mountain would guide him in his relations with the world of Guadalupe, here, so far from both their home together in Italy … and from his original mountain home.

A welcome tranquility enveloped him as he observed the approach of the distinguished man with two small children walking through the park toward the café leaving in their wake the mist of other days. Every day the gray-bearded man came with the children and stood on the other street side under a big Ash tree and looked toward the café sitters. Mystery hung over the man of about fifty with the two children of five or six years. Sometimes he treated the children to ices and they would stand there together under the great Ash tree looking fixedly but, Ethan sensed, unseeingly toward the café. Curiously, the man never crossed the street, but the usual café people knew him. Some would cross the street and speak a moment with him, discretely pressing something into his hand. The man was not a beggar and no one treated him as such. So Ethan had begun doing the same. Since he was still the only one at the café, he would chat a bit with the man he'd decided was a former university professor or had perhaps played a French horn in the city's symphony orchestra, and was now down on his luck.

Ethan bought ices for the children and he and the professor sat on a bench near the Coyotes Fountain and talked about Popocatepetl.

"But Professor, if Popo is invisible and no one can climb it, does the mountain really exist?" Looking in the direction of the mountains the idea again occurred to him that the secret of the end of time lay inside the toxic veil concealing Popocatepetl.

The man looked perplexed, then said in an erudite manner that he was not really a professor and that of course Popocatepetl existed. "It and its companion volcanoes, Iztaccihuatl and La Malinche, are always there. The Aztecs worshipped them like gods."

"Worshipped mountains, Professor? Well, some people worshiped the mountains where I came from, too ... but not my father."

The other fell silent, stroked the head of the little girl and wiped clean the boy's chin.

"Your children?" an envious Ethan asked.

"My grandchildren. Their mother died of pneumonia, the father vanished into Bidonville."

"Oh, how sad about your daughter. And Bidonville must be hell."

"Who knows? Anyway, Popocatepetl means Smoking Mountain and Iztaccihuatl, White Woman. According to an Aztec legend, they were once man and woman, deeply in love and were transformed into volcanic mountains. The third and less important mountain is La Malinche—named for an infamous woman who betrayed her people and became the mistress of Cortés the conquistador. The worst thing you can call a woman here is Malinche."

"Please tell me about it ... by the way were you a professor of history?"

"If you insist. Maybe yes, maybe no. Some things you know, other things you can only guess. Like the unicorn for example. I believe it exists. Anyway, I can tell you some things. First of all I assure you that Popocatepetl exists even though we cannot see it or climb it as Fidel and Che once did. As we know in this scientific age of atoms and viruses, invisibility does not mean non-existence ... as only simple-minded persons may think. Volcanic eruptions are eruptions. They happen. The most recent one was last January. They exist ... like the diseases the Spanish brought which killed the natives.

"In 1519 the Spanish conquerors arrived and erased the ancient Aztec culture that had passed its zenith. Moctezoma and his predecessors had ruled with Dostoevsky's three essential earthly forces: miracles, secrecy and rigid authority. Lacking however was the spontaneity of freedom so that after centuries cracks had begun showing in its structure and its civilization was crumbling. Consequently the Spanish victors wrote the history that became the truth for all time ... a history that paints the dreamy Aztec civilization as mere myth in the Mexican pantheon."

"Well the Spaniards' version has lasted. And that veil of fairytale and unreality still shrouds Western history of the Spanish conquest of what they found here."

"Oh yes, of course. Victors write the history. Still, solid Aztec sources tell another story of the conquest: on the onc hand, the breakdown of the Aztec network of uncertain alliances with the weaker peoples in its empire and, on the other, a creeping rottenness in Aztecisn which by then was a faith. But you have to keep in mind that even though it was disintegrating at the roots and in decline, it was an empire. Transitory in the passage of history, but still an empire. Moreover, total misunderstandings marked the ambivalent relations between the Spanish imperialists and the quixotic Mexica Aztecs who believed they could dominate the strange foreigners by a show of power ... and the usual bribery. Still, the Aztecs never understood that those men who didn't paint their bodies and wore armor had come to kill, conquer and loot Aztec gold. Men who sat atop four-legged beasts, the horses that would be deadly drones today. Men who took Aztec diplomatic gifts as weakness and killed the messengers. Men who had no honor and slaughtered women and children and destroyed whole villages. Men who had no such city of their own so they had to take the great sacred city of Tenochtitlan ..."

"They sound like my fellow countrymen!"

"Yes. The analogies are numerous. Anyway, though the Aztecs resisted, smallpox—invisible to the visionary Aztecs—broke out and masses of people in Tenochtitlan died from disease and starvation. Then before the year was out the Spanish rallied their forces here in Coyoacán and put Tenochtitlan under siege. At that point Aztec subject peoples shifted their alliances and joined the Spanish foreigners to crush the Aztecs in their city of gold. But against all odds the Aztecs still resisted so that the Spanish leveled the city with their cannons. And instead of a city of gold Spain took a city of rubble and the dead. The Aztec empire fell and its leader Moctezoma pulled down a nebulous civilization and its magical city with him. Now, as we know, such has been the ultimate fate of world empires."

"Professor, you have portrayed perfectly our shifting world today."

"Oh, that is neither here nor there."

"What do you mean, Sir?"

"I mean to say that it is a supreme example of the follies of mankind. But look at what happened to our Mexico. We have never again counted. Not since the time of Tenochtitlan has Mexico mattered. The Mexican-American war was a war of America against a fragile and weary Mexico. The monster of this brutal city we live in took the sacred city's place ... with the results we see every day. Poor Mexicans have hung onto their old gods and now have their ramshackle Bidonville while the rich white Spaniards can live in great *palacios* in protected districts of the city and crush the poor without ever having seen them. Gibbons wrote that 'Such is the constitution of civil society, that whilst a few persons are distinguished by riches, by honors, and by knowledge, the body of the people is condemned to obscurity, ignorance and poverty. In *The Decline and Fall of the Roman Empire* he wrote: 'A long period of distress and anarchy, in which empire, and arts, and riches had migrated from the banks of the Tiber was incapable of restoring or adorning the city; and, as all that is human must retrograde if it does not advance, every successive age must have hastened the ruin of the works of antiquity.'"

"Professor, you know my homeland well!"

"Alas, I truly do. The old saying about Mexico's ills still holds: *Pobre Mexico tan lejos de dios y tan cerca de los Estados Unidos.* Poor Mexico, so far from God and so near the United States. For there is no better place than Mexico to see first-hand the negative results of the pact between American capitalism and the tiny elite classes of society that exploits the country's hard-working people. In Old Mexico, the *past* is the future. For our indigeneous peoples progress is a return to the pre-Aztec past. I mean to say that the Golden Age for Mexicans is in the remote past. Utopia for Mexicans means a return to their origins and to the original time of ancient civilizations. Yet if Mexico like Popocatepetl is invisible to much of the world, we are still here and Mexico exists."

"Well, though the Aztec empire fell, Aztecism remains. The Spanish world empire fell too, but imperialism remains. We keep repeating the same mistakes."

"The things of man are indeed fragile. The Aztecs are gone but their sacred Popocatepetl remains, roaring and blasting its lava to warn us, and we can't even see it … it has its lava but we have our pollution."

Ethan pressed an envelope into the other's hands. "Something nice for the children," he said. "Uh, Professor, I just got the idea of looking for your son-in-law in Bidonville. Maybe he needs help. What's his name?"

"Name? Well, he's called Juan Carlos Morelos. About thirty-five. Looks older, I'm sure. Sickly type. Tall and skinny."

"I hope to see you again tomorrow, Sir."

"Tomorrow as every day. Coming here is our job," he said with an embarrassed smile. Little children already working! It's shameful."

"Maybe I've found a job, too."

2.

Ethan's taxi zigzagged through a web of streets, entered a traffic-packed avenue and pulled to a stop in front of a block of structures covered in Coca Cola placards. Just behind them spread rows of tin and cardboard shacks, each different in shape and material. One was painted pink and ecologically green. 'So this is it', he muttered. 'Bidonville, Mexico City.'

Night was descending over Mexico City when Ethan stepped inside Bidonville. Abruptly a sudden blackness fell over the world. Since he had no plan he stumbled through the darkness searching for a light and feeling like an alien from another planet. Ankle deep in slime and overpowered by the stench, he marveled at the sensation: he felt free. Freer here in his aloneness than in Coyoacán. He seemed to see himself. You need this kind freedom to find yourself. You need the courage to accept your freedom when you find it. If not, you feel death. He felt giddy. It was his rogue freedom. This was the total isolation from Guadalupe he'd needed. Like a hermit must feel. Still, he thought, it takes as much courage to be a hermit as to be a heretic. Even though surrounded by European ghosts, he felt he was on the right path, maybe dangerous but the right one. But what if this is hallucination? Can a Bidonville really exist in one of the world's biggest cities? If I'm not careful my mind and body and my soul will transform into a Bidonville. And then in that very moment, salvation. He saw a light far down the alley.

Hesitantly he entered the shack. Candles were spaced around an unexpectedly spacious room. Mud from the earlier rain seeped inside under his feet. Mosquitoes buzzed around his head. Something snapped in his reeling mind and an ambiguous reality returned when out of the shadows a young man stepped forward.

"Hola, I'm Marcos. I'm helping out here." Ethan's eyes continued darting around the space. Layers of cardboard covered much of the earthen floor. Along the tin walls, crates of milk, dried foods, labeled bags and piles of big blue bottles of drinking water. A cot and red blankets.

"Donations," Marcos said. The man in his middle twenties was white, European-looking, well-spoken, wearing mud-caked pants. "But never enough for the thousands of people here."

"Did the city send you out here?"

"The city? Why Mexico City doesn't know Bidonville even exists. That is, it knows … but it doesn't know. The rich never look this way. And the good bourgeoisie doesn't want to know of the existence of this other city. This is a parallel city, invisible to the others. Bidonville City exists only because TV reporters film it from helicopters. And because police raid it every time there is a drug-related killing in the area."

"Are there really drug gangs here?"

"People here are more likely victims than pushers. Say, you're not police, are you? You don't have that look. But drug cartels and their pushers? No, I don't think so. Anyway, can I help you?"

"I'm looking for the father of some small children I know. His name is Juan Carlos Morelos. About thirty-five, tall and thin and sickly."

"Everybody here looks sickly. But not many tall and thin men. Most squat and tiny. But wait a minute! We'll see."

From the opening, Marcos whistled sharply. Moments later two dark brown boys of eleven or twelve ran up the alley. Marcos confabulated with them and they ran off.

"My intelligence organization," he explained. "If Juan Carlos is here, they'll find him."

"Maybe you need some help here. I can contribute some supplies."

"You want to help here? Nobody dares even enter here. But of course, you're ..."

Suddenly a tall shadow dressed in baggy dirty brown pants and shirt had filled the entrance way.

"I'm Morelos," he said, eyeing Ethan suspiciously.

It happened so fast that Ethan didn't know what to say. Then: "I know your children. They need you."

"I have no children. I have no one ... not in this world."

"You have Nella and you have Juanito, a father-in-law, and now you have me. You have more people in this world than I do. I only want to climb Popocatepetl. Breathe some good air. All of us need it."

The man stared at Ethan as if he were *loco como una cabra*. Dressed like a foreigner, visiting him in this hell hole ... and wants to go mountain climbing, he had to be crazy as hell.

"I couldn't take care of them. My wife, Laurita ... she died. She was real life. I had a job in our hometown ... in Puebla. And we had our children. But there's the dirt, the dust, and she got sick. With her gone, I began dying too. *Los niños* are better off with Laurita's *padre*."

"Oh, he loves them. Everyone in Coyoacán loves them. But children need their father ... oh God, look at that!" Ethan exclaimed pointing toward a huge rat sitting on its haunches near the sacks and looking at them with glistening eyes. "It's as big as a cat."

"Oh, that's Caesar," Marcos said picking up an iron rod and moving toward the beast. “No cats in Bidonville. The rats eat them, too. Caesar thinks he lives here. I leave grain on a plate for him so he doesn’t attack the sacks of corn meal.” When the rat saw the rod, he watched Marcos for a moment as if to determine if he meant business, then judiciously scampered toward them, passed just next to Juan Carlos and out the door.

All three of them then winced at the sudden whining of sirens. Red and yellow lights swept over the swamp of darkness. Leapfrogging searchlights from a helicopter swept up and down the flooded alleys separating the irregular rows of sheds and lean-tos and inundated the room with distorted pale shapes. They heard the police cars ramming shacks. At each thud of metal against cardboard and tin, Marcos and Juan Carlos shuddered, waiting for the crumbling sound of another structure collapsing over someone’s head.

“Lots of action today! Still, Bidonville is forever fugitive,” a depressed Marcos said, sitting down on a bench along a wall, his hands hanging helplessly between his legs. “It expands and shrinks like a dirty giant accordion according to the season and police interventions. Garbage and excrement bob on the black waters in the alleys steeped in slime. Mud crawls everywhere, cold and sticky at night, stinking and fly-infested during the day. Mud seeps under my cardboard door that I prop up at night. But it’s an uneven battle against the filth. Living here inside the reality of Bidonville, I fear I also forget real pity. Nobody pities anybody here.”

Ethan slapped at the mosquitoes buzzing in his ears, nose and mouth despite the spirals burning in each corner. Juan Carlos stood near the entrance, expressionless as if he didn’t count. Marcos rambled: “Bidonville inhabitants get used to the mosquitoes and the smells but many are bronchitic or tubercular because of the dampness and the night chill at this altitude. From here it’s hard to imagine that you are even in gigantic Mexico City ... that you really exist. Here inside the labyrinth, reality is illusory.

“It’s not the noise and chaos of Mexico that’s remarkable here: it’s the quiet. Nights you can hear the grunts in the darkness of human beings making love. Early today an anonymous tip signaled two bodies dumped in a ditch inside the perimeter of Bidonville. A police journalist told me drug lords had assassinated two rival dealers. So police are imparting a lesson to Bidonville as if it were responsible.

"Bidonville has to be the bottom of the world ... where the rejects of the visible world gather. But it itself is an invisible world. Its inhabitants are invisible … or they exist only in their dreams. Though they might dream of a better life, day-by-day real life slips through their fingers. When I walk in the dark alleyways, a chill creeps down my spine and I flick my flashlight to scare away the very real and visible rats. Yet, though most people here are poor in imagination of a better life, some few are rich in a kind of innate brilliance. A few make it! There might be an Einstein here!"

New clothes and a shower in Ethan's Coyoacán.rooms, and Juan Carlos was a new man. Dressed in khaki and with clean black hair, though still extremely pale there was something special about him, curiosity reawakening in his black eyes. A descendant of the Toltecs, Ethan decided. Known for their immaculate ways, their wisdom, the clarity of their speech, Toltecs were artistic and also great warriors. Bidonville had nearly eradicated those characteristics but the real Juan was reviving. Maybe, Ethan imagined, he's destined to be a great writer … or a realist painter.

Juan's curious eyes swept over the café on the plaza as if he were meeting the West for the first time. Ethan saw in the scene confirmation that Mexico is Western … and it is not. In Mexico City you see Western civilization. But in the dances of the Concheros on Plaza Mayor he'd seen reflections of the other Mexico to which Juan Carlos belonged. Though the number of indigenous people is still great and most speak Spanish today, they remain the mysterious forefathers of the Aztecs, descendants of pre-historic peoples who crossed the Bering Strait from Siberia and drifted southwards along the shores of another world. Yet, contradictorily, Mexico is more Spanish than countries like Argentina or Chile with their German and Italian immigrants. Mexico is a country between two civilizations—one Western, the other indigenous—and between two pasts—one Spanish and the other pre-Hispanic. In his *El Laberinto de la Soledad,* Octavio Paz writes that just as behind the

Greeks stood the Egyptians or behind the Romans stood the Etruscans, behind the Aztecs and the Spanish conquerors who formed today's Mexicans there stand millennia of peoples in a long and dizzying past. Mexico is different. People on this plateau have always been different. Aztecs emphasized their otherness—in their language and dress, and in their strange culture including human sacrifice. Ghoulish priests covered in blood cutting out human hearts on the killing stones at the top of their pyramids. They *wanted* to be different. Spartan people too, they considered others inferior, stupid and comical.

"We'll be here tomorrow when your children and father-in-law come," Ethan promised. Juan smiled when Ethan added: "They always stand just across the street under that Ash tree."

3.

Lermontov wrote of flowers which the more you look after them, the less they respond to your efforts. Such had become Ethan's relationship with his wife, Guadalupe. The more he loved her, the more distant she became. And he suffered from her absences. He had given up his old way of life and moved to her country to care for the woman he loved, leaving his job in Europe and accepting the minor role in their relationship. His new status could have been humiliating. But it was not. It was his existential priority that had changed. His new role in his still undetermined life was dedicated to his "Lupe".

In their early years together in Italy, beautiful Guadalupe with her long dark hair was angelic. But today back in her homeland she had acquired the bewildering capacity to transform into a demon. Maybe her transfiguration had to do with the ancient history of the Mexico City suburb where they lived. Coyoacán—place of the coyotes—built on the site of a pre-Colombian settlement from which the Spanish conquistador Hernán Cortés launched that final attack on Tenochtitlan. The dream city fell to the Spaniards and became Mexico City.

Ethan loved Coyoacán. He loved walking by Frida Kahlo's Blue House just around the corner from the café. Life's satisfactions were no longer measured according to the same standards he'd known before. Life seemed to have reached a higher plateau, even though he sensed that its finest qualities still escaped him. In any case, position and influence no longer existed as values. And now if he had less of Lupe, he had his extended family to care for: Juan Carlos, two children and their grandfather. Still, his life in this new Old World was nonetheless frustrating because of that one great shortcoming in his new world: Guadalupe was no longer the loving woman she'd once been.

He was truly puzzled. Were they no longer the same people? It seemed less a question of place than he'd thought—whether in Italy where they'd lived those years, or here in her family house in the historic center of Coyoacán—but of the length of their time together and their proximity one to the other. And he recalled the old adage: 'familiarity breeds contempt.'

Now Ethan's existential situation was indeed peculiar. He spoke the language but the country where he'd re-settled was a hazy unknown. He'd always spoken Spanish with Lupe and he'd been here with her on short visits. But visits were one thing, permanent residence another. It was strange to hear what in Italy had been their somewhat secret language spoken everywhere.

Even the flight from Europe to Mexico several months earlier was different … this time a one-way trip. From the high skies Ethan had perceived the approach to the triangle of Mexico as a metaphysical happening. After overflying the Rio Grande the earthen mass below seemed to rise upwards toward the heavens. Mountainous ridges swelled and tumbled forward from western skies like great oceanic waves. And his past too skipped away across spinning gossamer clouds. Invisible worlds zoomed around him. Mexico narrowed and the sky retreated heavenwards. And the bluish mountains filling the triangular plateau called Mesoamerica formed a gigantic pyramid surrounded by the seas. It was the top of the world, where time stood still. He'd felt a sensation of dizzying power and the mystery of the unknown.

Ethan too had wanted the move. His conviction that it was time to go beyond Italy and Europe had changed his orientation. Moving to Mexico must be like he imagined going to war used to be for young men—escape from the dead-end-you of home when your hopes begin to decline and your dreams fade and you are ready to do any mad thing to survive. Their transfer to Mexico was a move toward a new form of sanity in a disordered world, for Ethan an attempt to get a handle on life. To acquire a generalized awareness. A consciousness of everything. But he now realized that was utopistic thinking … in a way more terrible than his usual out-of-tuneness and solitude.

Now, again, for his very survival in this new life he had to change his whole existence. Again, undertake something new. Reestablish a healthy spatial distance between Guadalupe and himself as his work had done in Italy. A buffer zone could save them. He had to isolate a block of time and space for himself. A time during which he could become a separate entity, independent of Lupe and her world.

He accepted that in every couple one loves more than the other. And since he was the one whose love—and dependence—was the greater, he suffered more from the widening distance between them, while Lupe seemed indifferent to his absences. Missing in his lonely world had long been a genuine passion that was not Guadalupe. She had her world; he still had to construct his. So he'd set about creating *his* space. Now he had a lost Toltec in his charge. He had another family that needed him. Nevertheless, he still suffered disorientation. Anxiety. Strange new impulses like his fixation on Popcatepetl drove him.

Marcos in Bidonville had said that people in one district of this city never knew what people in other parts were doing—twenty-five million people? Thirty million? No one knew. A mystery. The city's immensity truly merited a gigantic volcanic mountain with the fitting name of Popocatepetl or Smoking Mountain even if it remained hidden from view. Shy today, he thought, one day Popo will reveal itself.

An experienced urban explorer, Ethan had walked and tabulated New York, Paris and Rome. So he made plotting this gigantic city part of his new space. A challenging venture when he saw that as Marcos warned for people of suburban Coyoacán the center of the Old City at Plaza Mayor was like a foreign country. People in western parts of the city knew nothing of the eastern districts. Though some days he wandered randomly around the city too huge to see whole, clearly

Mexico City-Tenochtitlan existed. It was visible ... just not as a whole. And people in one part of the city didn't know what was happening in the other parts. Its peoples—battling traffic, assuring personal security, drunk on weekends and fighting for physical survival—showed no signs of knowing what life was about. The great Valley of Mexico seemed like the final stage of the madness of civilized man, suspended between the rich West and the Fourth World. Nowhere even a basis for optimism. He would unite this disunited city ... conceptually: he set out to walk the length of *Insurgentes*, the great avenue that formed a 28.8 kilometer long north-south axis dividing the city into two halves like Broadway in Manhattan. Plodding northwards through the once unusual heavy mists, kilometers of slim colored glass skyscraper skies hung over him. Old Tenochtitlan was the vanguard of modernity; Mexico itself a political caveman ... a capitalist semi-dictatorship based on corruption and retention of power. He rushed through underpasses and around traffic circles sucking in the carbon monoxide of incessant traffic. The white marble of the Bellas Artes Museum didn't ameliorate the pollution or calm Mexico's dust. Nor did the dainty delicacies of Sanborn's restaurants or Starbucks or the revolutionary murals of Siquieros, Rivera and Orozco make the water potable. The delightful spring temperatures didn't freshen smog-filled throats. And the blasé rich in Zona Rosa restaurants ignored the withered women on the streets rationing tortillas to tiny children. A tragic country lay behind its pieces. It was Mexico's ancient origins ... and its solitude on its highlands and in its jungles.

But, somehow, Mexico is not decadent as were the Aztecs at the time of the mystical arrival of the Spanish conquistadors. Mexico can rise again. A viable society of young ambitious people, a country on its way up. At one point on Insurgentes Nord he was half singing, half reciting '*Round like a circle in a spiral... a wheel within a wheel ... an ever spinning reel ... a tunnel that you follow to a tunnel of its own ...* when he heard jazz from a bar identified as Bar Americano. He stopped at an open window to listen. Music of the past: Dave Brubeck, he thought. He hummed along. The radio DJ announced they'd just heard *Poor Butterfly* ... and then translated the title as *Pobre Mariposa*. Ethan thought *Poor Butterfly* more romantically melancholy.

He added the Bar Americano and the song titles to his notes in which he listed names of streets and buildings and bus stations and museums and restaurants, accumulating a mass of unrelated raw data ... but he never succeeded in linking in his mind the illogical divisions of the city and never reached the north end of the endless *avenida*.

If little besides hope remains of the Great Revolution in this country the size of Italy and France together, he came to believe that something *is* going on under the surface of Mexico's social fabric that could reemerge as happened in Bolivia and Venezuela, something enormous, something as powerful and unstoppable as the winds sweeping down from the north.

4.

Juan Carlos moved into the apartment with his children and father-in-law, Victor Ibarra Villalobos. It was the first floor of a two-story house near the Frida Kahlo Blue House Museum, an apartment that a Coyoacán social organization had awarded him years earlier for unspecified outstanding services to the community. Ethan still called Victor "Professor", who although he never acknowledged that he was once a history professor, he knew a lot about many things ranging from ancient Mexico to the socio-political sciences. Victor Ibarra's contacts among the café crowd—of whom many were influential persons in the township—succeeded in creating for Juan Carlos the position of gardener of the communal park opposite the café. Ethan's relations with the new family were close, their house his second home. The children danced around him in expectation of the red and green ices he brought and they called him *Tio Etan*. And Juan Carlos always said: "*Mi casa es tu casa.*

And then there appeared posters and signs around the Coyoacán center announcing lectures by Professor Victor Ibarra Villalobos in the township auditorium.

"Well!" Ethan exclaimed, suppressing a mild reproof of Victor's reticence about his background. "Who are you?"

"It's complicated," Victor said softly, spreading his hands as if in regret of a whole life ... but without further explanations. "We'll see after the two talks I will present."

"We'll see what?"

"We'll see where we go from here."

Victor's public lectures were sensational events. The auditorium was packed. Juan Carlos, Juanito, Nella and Ethan had the best seats in the front row together with communal dignitaries, academics and intellectuals all apparently eager to hear Professor Ibarra's well-known lessons again. Ethan became aware of a certain nostalgia pervading the front rows as if for the return from exile of a prodigal son. People were unusually attentive. Little chatter was heard before Professor Ibarra stepped from the wings, greeted by a ripple of a hesitant applause. Ethan was mystified. Where had Victor been? What had he done to alienate himself for perhaps years?

"I will begin at the end," were Victor's first words at which someone just behind Ethan said softly: "Hurrah!" "But first I extend my gratitude to those true friends who made this my, umm, my return possible. You know who you are as do I.

"This evening however I have decided to risk all—again—and send an oral message to Andrés Manuel Lopez Obrador, Mexico's President. 'Despite many warnings—including mine—Amlo, as we call you, you made the pilgrimage to Washington and signed also in my name a meaningless trade pact. The first step toward another surrender. I warned you, dear President, many times: Do not go, Amlo. But you went. Do not go, Amlo, I warned. Do not drink the Kool Aid, Amlo. Do not eat the forbidden fruit, Amlo. But you went and drank and ate. Do not let yourself be branded with the mark of the beast, Amlo. But you did. And you are now branded, Amlo. Therefore the curse will now pour upon us Mexicans. Accursed by the Spanish, now accursed again and again and again by the Yankees. Doom hangs heavy over us. When the empire of all empires in Washington falls, so will our beloved Mexico fall, again.'

"Dear friends I cannot help but think of Tezcatlipoca that terrible eagle god of ancient Mexicans who is still alive for many of us. God of the gods, the unpredictable god of human destiny, who continually erupts in the lives of his creations. In his obsidian mirror Tezcatlipoca sees dreamlike images of the deeds of men on earth and obscure visions of future events. Like Yahweh, capricious Tezcatlipoca praises men one moment and punishes them the next. He makes life on earth a dream, and then from another dream creates another life. In the mad god's vision we're fleeting and insignificant.

"The Norteamericanos are today a vanishing people. An egotistic and narcissist people. But our history shows that we Mexicans are a universal people. On the other hand, the reality of Mexican destiny makes you wonder if it's positive to be so universal that you can accept *anything* philosophically. For no more than has its toxic proximity to the USA, universality has not brought great fortune to Mexico. It seems that only the most ancient peoples are capable of being simply men. Men who don't strive for perfection and just lead good lives are universal without realizing it. It makes them free ... but at the same time vulnerable to the claws of the hawks."

5.

Professor Ibarra's two speeches stirred up considerable talk among the café crowd. He still came each afternoon, now to the café itself, as a rule with Ethan or as the guest of one or another. An "Ibarra circle" was forming. And the aura of mystery about him thickened. Many words had been spoken about Amlo's Washington trip and the expected long-range ramifications for Mexico itself. The border wall was still on people's minds, which the more cynical believed Mexico would end up paying for. According to some of the café people Lopez Obrador had detailed reports on Ibarra's dire forecasts for the homeland. Ethan was then surprised to learn that Ibarra and the President were former "comrades". Yet, while Ibarra vanished into oblivion Lopez Obrador went on to become the leader of the national center-left party and now President of the Republic. More Mexican mysteries.

One day as they strolled through the park toward the café, Ethan on an impulse stopped Victor and suggested they taxi to an unusual bar in an unexpected place: the Gran Hotel in the city center. Victor looked at him in a funny way but nodded. When Ethan said he'd long wanted to see it, Victor just shrugged and after a hesitation gracefully slid into the taxi. This man, Ethan thought, so elegant in spirit and movement, now sitting so composed and self-assured, truly possesses those unusual qualities that he found himself imitating. Chatting about one thing or the other along Avenida Insurgentes, the song in the Bar Americano came to mind. He knew Victor spoke perfect English even though he avoided using it, so he asked which title he preferred, *Poor Butterfly* or *Pobre Mariposa.*

"Oh, that song goes far back. I know it as *Poor Butterfly* which I prefer. The song writer had a real duende that you don't hear in the title *Pobre Mariposa.*"

Ethan stared at him in surprise. "Is there anything you don't know?" he asked, truly flabbergasted.

"I've lived a full life ... in many places. What can you expect?"

"Then you surely know the Gran Hotel de la Ciudad de Mexico?"

"I've heard of it. But I've never been there either. An old hotel, dating back centuries, to before the United States of North America was born ... famous for its Art Nouveau canopy. Well, so that's the surprise! Just as well!"

And the interior was breath-robbing: four stories and a canopy of Tiffany stained glass art. They sat on a balcony of the third floor bar overlooking the art nouveau splendor. They sipped mojitos.

"A remembrance of times past," Victor murmured. When Ethan asked which times, Victor told him all: "My father, Manuel Ibarra, was a leader of the student protests in 1968 against the huge sums spent on the Olympic Games that year in Mexico while people lived in poverty. He penned the slogan *No queremos Olimpiadas, queremos revolución.* When the army opened fire on the ten thousand students gathered on La Plaza de las Tres Culturas, they killed hundreds of students including my father. The army stacked the bodies for all to see on the square, over a thousand some said. The only crime of the dead was agitation. I grew up with that memory. When decades later I spoke about it ... against the same corrupt political system, they exiled me. I went to Cuba. Then to France and finally to the USA. And now I'm back! All of that is packed in my message to President Lopez Obrador ... our dear Amlo."

A few weeks passed. October was ending. The daily mists grew heavier, nuanced, at times taking on eerie shades of yellow and green.

Every day Ethan checked the skies with ever lessening optimism for a visible sign of the presence of Popocatepetl. One evening in the café he again proposed to Juan Carlos a hike up the trails of the Smoking Mountain.

"You have holidays next week. Let's go now. Bad weather will soon arrive."

"Popo is closed to hikers. Too dangerous. Eruptions are still predicted. You know that story."

"Juan Carlos, you lived in Puebla, practically under Popo so you must know the secret trails … the uncontrolled ones. The crater is 5,426 meters high. The map shows we can drive to the Paso de Cortes and on to Tlamacas at about 3,000 meters. I promise that if we hear any rumbles we'll just drive away. Now you know this best but hikers' guides calculate it's only a six-hour walk to the top. Think about it, Juan, the top of the world! And we'll know it's really there."

"Oh, it's there, Ethan. I've been there. It's there. But it's forbidden. Why don't you just go with an organized tourist group?"

"What! A tourist jaunt! Why that's insulting, *amigo mio*. Besides, it's not only to make sure Popocatepetl is there. Listen, Juan Carlos. I've just got to get to the top of the world. I have to. Just one time."

"They organize hikes in Puebla, too," Juan Carlos added weakly. "It's the easiest."

"Yes, but they won't go up Popocatepetl. It's forbidden."

"Yes, forbidden. But they will take you up Iztaccihuatl and you can see Popo perfectly."

"And also La Malinche. But that's not the same thing, you know that, Juan Carlos. Not the same thing at all."

"No, *de acuerdo*, that's not the same thing."

"You have to understand that it's not only to make sure it's there. Listen, my friend, you've been there. Maybe many times. You're a Toltec. You know many things. Maybe you know what the top of the world is like. Now I have to know, too. I've just got to get to the top of the world. I have to. Just one time."

"No, looking at Popocatepetl from Iztaccihuatl or Malinche is not the same as climbing Popo," Juan Carlos repeated.

Ethan looked at his friend closely. It was hard to remember that only a few months ago he'd been withering away in Bidonville. Now he was nearly convinced to go with him on this mad mountain climbing jaunt.

"Ok," Ethan said. "You can go as far as Tlamacas. Then I'll walk to the top alone. I don't mind going to the top of the world alone. Not at all."

Ethan turned and waved at the Toltec standing now with his hands on his hips and a false smile on his pale narrow face. Juan Carlos lifted one arm in a weak salute and sat back down on the straight chair he'd placed in front of the abandoned lodge. Ethan knew he would sit there to await his return in that tranquil immobility of which only ancient peoples are capable. He was encouraged that Juan Carlos had understood that reaching the very top was a matter of existential significance for him: he understood that Ethan had no choice. But all that hardly mattered now that he was on his way to the summit. The top of the world.

Ethan looked upwards and smiled: the dense pine forest was pleasant like a cool appetizer at lunchtime on a hot day in the Rome countryside. Wait, was that a chill he felt? No matter. He zipped up the light sweater he'd started with. The traces of the trail worn by the many feet before him were still visible though now nearly erased by liberated vegetation. He thought that even when the trail one day became invisible it would still exist and in some future it would re-live and carry others to the top of the world.

When the trees began thinning, he felt a surprising but still pleasant coldness despite the exertion of the climb. Then, when he passed the last trees of the timberline, he stopped to gape at the vast Alpine meadows opening before him.

And when he again stopped for his first unobstructed view of Popocatepetl, he felt a slight earth tremor and heard the low intensity explosions above him. Aggressively though reverently he accelerated his pace upwards across the meadows. His urban hikes had prepared him for this physical endurance test. And he suspected it was the ecstasy like that of heretics singing glory to God while burning at the stake that made him insensitive to fatigue, cold and pain.

Once he was above the meadows explosions arising from the depths rocked the very earth under his feet. It seemed the whole world was in movement. As he began the last leg of the climb, he looked up at the summit and smiled when he felt the ash falling on his shoulders. He was much higher than five thousand meters. He sang and hummed under his breath words from an old song … *Like the circles that you find in the windmills of your mind! Dah, dah, dah … And the world is like an apple whirling silently in space … Like the circles that you find ….*

“Wait, wait, I’m arriving!” he shouted. There were no tunnels in his mind. No caverns. He was at the top. He no longer felt the cold but put on another sweater and a skull cap anyway.

Subsequent explosions and smoke plumes only excited him more. He had reached the summit of the world; it justified, and destroyed, his life.

RECONCILIATIONS

Max and Greta agreed that everyone needs two main dramas in their lives, one in their public life and the other in their private space. Max said that his public drama as a political journalist provided him a place where he felt right, so that he didn't have to blow his brains out each day because of his endless fuck-ups in his private life. Greta's public life in an advertising agency gave her personal satisfaction because she believed she injected honesty into a field peopled by liars. But she, too, had misgivings about her private life where it was one mistake after the other. Both considered their lives balancing acts between their complex private lives as opposed to their flawless public personae.

A life-changing disaster had begun on a rainy night in a penthouse studio near Piazza di Spagna. Until midnight to the pleasant rhythm of the pitter-pattering of a steady rainfall on the flagstone terraces lining the sides of the artist's apartment, Greta Dovidio and her friend, the painter Maria-Teresa, had chatted about love and drank moderately; Greta's fiancé, Massimiliano Pane—or Max—drank less moderately and spoke more animatedly than usual with their Swedish adventuress friend named Ellinor who drank excessively.

There was nothing unusual about Ellinor's exhibition, but the sultry Swede had just broken up with another exhausted boyfriend and was either grieving or celebrating their separation, which encouraged her seduction vice and endangered the easily seduced Max whom she'd had in her sights that entire calamitous evening.

"Love!" Ellinor sneered—her eyes fixed sexily on Max. "Who invented the word, Plato? Love is a euphemism. A reason to quaff the stuff in this glass and have all the sex we want. Anything to help us overcome our loneliness."

For Greta, tonight's sequence of events was another sign of Max's weak character; for Max it was a regrettable but insignificant episode in their social life. He blamed what happened on the wine and beer and the cold vodka, his malleable character and the aggressive Swedish blond who drank like a sailor on shore-leave in Veracruz and fucked any fuckable male at hand.

So, when they drove the drunken nympho home, gallant Max escorted her to her door while Greta waited in the car. When he kissed her on each cheek in the Italian good-night manner, she in a sudden move yanked him inside her foyer where in about three minutes she raped him in the Swedish good-night manner without leaving her feet. On Max's disappearance behind the Swede's front door, a furious Greta had responded in typical Greta manner: she drove away locked in first gear just as she'd left him locked in the arms of the Swedish lush. At home, she again hurled armloads of his belongings out the window into the rain. Then she locked the entrance door, put in ear plugs and went to bed.

What had happened before, happened again. Max walked the three miles home in the rain, the whole time drunkenly obsessing about Greta's recurrent nightmare of imaginary buzzards pecking her eyes. Her terror was being locked in a small room with a flock of dirty black buzzards flapping around her head. He felt certain her hallucinations had delusional significance and caused her brutal treatment of him.

From the wet street under their bedroom windows, Max's own craziness erupted as he shouted for Greta to open their fucking door. He was sick of her insane behavior and her buzzards. He drinks a bit too much and some Swedish vamp comes on to him, and Greta goes nuts as if those buzzards really existed. Leaves him outside in the rain where he would catch pneumonia. All her fault that he was so tired and hoarse, and coughing and sneezing. So he yelled louder and louder for Greta to open their fucking door.

Like other times, neighbors' windows begin banging open, men and women with maddened faces shook their fists and shouted the usual threats of calling the police or the fire department, their shouts reverberating up and down the narrow street.

Between his now muted calls of 'Greta, Greta, Greta', Max began gathering his soggy stuff spread over the wet sidewalk and pushing what fit pell-mell into his trusty old suitcase that Greta had thoughtfully provided.

At the acme of his drunken furor and his ache for his Greta, other windows of their palazzo opened. The inhabitants were familiar with Max and Greta's torrid relationship. In fact, the couple was part of the lore of the wild apartment palazzo at number one of Via Calcata (named after a trendy old township north of the city), a street Greta called Via Calvario because of their suffering there; Max named it Via Calcutta for the same reason.

"Quiet! Enough you two! Basta!" a lady on the fourth floor yelled.

"Oh, God, just listen to that racket. Those two are at it again." "And to think that they're the two most beautiful people in the city," someone insisted.

"They do it all the time," another shouted.

"But why their endless fighting?" someone asked. "Why don't they divorce if they can't live together?"

"God knows what holds those two together?" echoed the answers.

"Love!" responded the ancient philosopher from the top floor and closed quietly his window to them all ... like God speaking to mankind, Max thought.

After a moment of respectful silence from all the windows, the philosopher's immediate neighbor seconded the old man: "Truly theirs is a great love."

"I don't believe they know how great their love is," a fat man in an undershirt from a fifth floor window door added.

"Love is the most beautiful thing in the world."

"And the love of two such beautiful people," the same voice remarked.

"I'm a marriage counselor," shouted a shrill vice from just below the philosopher's window. "Let the children come unto me."

"Are they even married?" a little old lady asked, whom no one answered. "Love!" the sarcastic divorcée in the fourth floor window repeated like a mantra the philosopher's conclusion.

"They can't live apart," another noted.

"Ah, this new generation," said a saintly voice through a turret from the basement apartment. "No morality at all."

Exasperated, Max shouted drunkenly, "Thass the lass straw, and will you juss fuck off, Priest!" To which he added a "Forgive me, Father, for I have sinned!"

After the mention of *love*, the yelling and the cursing and the epithets and the calls for police had subsided and finally ceased. And silence came to reign over the palazzo in Via Calcata.

A soberer Max found a stray key to the palazzo door and lugged up the stairs the now soggy suitcase and assorted wet stuff, piled it all against his apartment door and as usual settled on the floor.

At five-thirty a.m. he was shaken awake, cracked his eyes and met those of the *portiere* making his rounds. "The usual, Dottore?" the older man asked in irony and pulled out an enormous key ring and jangled it under Max's nose.

"Of course," Max whispered.

The Super unlocked his door and with his help Max dragged his stuff inside and collapsed onto the heavenly living room couch, his last thought lingering that 'the drinks and the stand-up fuck just weren't worth the candle.'

Massimiliano Pane and Greta Dovidio had been together for three years. Their love affair had been fervent from the start … their separations no less so. Each time Massimiliano was humiliated and rabid; Greta, indignant and miserable. You go your way and I go mine, was their resolution. Distance, loneliness and isolation, the outcome. And then reconciliation. Their separations lasted about thirty-six hours. This time Max slept on the couch also the following night before the next morning rejoining her in their boudoir and falling into her open arms. Those two just couldn't stay apart.

A week or so later, on a crystal-clear November day they were walking to the supermarket when Max stopped, his head turned toward the skies. "Look at that, Greta. A good luck sign. It's like we're lying in a field of white and yellow flowers on a warm August day and watching flocks of birds flying northwards to their mysterious destinations while we earthlings speak fearlessly of our present as accomplished. We know where we're going, together."

The sky was suddenly darkened by hundreds of thousands of gyrating birds, dark masses, swelling and shrinking, inhaling and exhaling like breathing lungs. Starling scouts rocketed earthwards in search of landing places in the stone city. It was the winter migration of millions of European starlings who love the mild winter weather of Rome. They come for days, maybe weeks, sometimes months. And they love the cement of the city itself, the stone embankments along the river where Greta would never go. They were all buzzards for her.

Observing the arrival of the birds, Greta had the thought that also the lives of successful families were marked by regular recurrences and repetition like that of the migratory birds. Birthdays and marriages and the birth of children proceeded according to fixed codes. 'But Max and I have no core. Nothing to which to belong … besides our love. But that is not a tangible object to hold onto. Maybe a sacrament like marriage would serve us well.

"Yes, Max, you are right in so many things. Finally we're getting used to each other's quirks and weaknesses."

"Right, my love. Like I worry less today about your conviction of the dangers of the full moon and your fears of the buzzards."

"Now Max, don't exaggerate. Some things are too much. I still can't accept the assurances of your soberness when you can hardly walk across the room without falling into the arms of some wanton Scandinavian."

"Well, er, Greta, you know too that things are not always what they seem."

"Now what the fuck does that mean, as the drunken Swedish whore would say? Sometimes they are exactly what they seem."

"Yes, but … Hey, Greta, watch! Let's watch this performance in the heavens … just for us. Maybe the starlings are celebrating our marriage."

Soon the Swedish mishap never seemed to have occurred. One afternoon the happy couple, hand-in-hand, Greta never letting go

Massimiliano's hand, ran into the priest walking down Via Calcata, his arms full of groceries, the necks of several wine bottles showing from one sack.

"Well," said the frocked one, "the happy children, Massimiliano and Greta, the love and joy and suffering of our whole palazzo. How good to see you like this in the glory of God's smile."

"Thank you, Father," Max said, always respectful to men of the cloth, of whose words he didn't believe even a comma. "You are too kind to two of God's stray children! We have decided to follow God's command: we're getting married."

So a short while later the whole palazzo population joined the couple's friends, relatives and co-workers for their civil wedding in the City Hall Red Room on the Capitoline Hill that looked to Max and Greta suspiciously like a church.

'My vision is now clear,' Max thought as the merry group of the celebrants walked down from the Capitoline hill to a wedding lunch. 'Where then was our waywardness? Oh, fucking Christ—so sorry, Father!—the blindness of the self-righteous who think a marriage license changes anything. Do I feel different since the Mayor's representative said 'I pronounce you, Massimiliano, and you, Greta, man and wife? No, I do not. Marriage is not enough. Greta and I must keep in mind that marriage is often just another wall to separate lovers and destroy love, as the sixth-floor philosopher so wisely said. It is not a bridge as the third floor marriage counselor and the basement priest claim.

'But then, what about love? So where does love go when it departs in a time in which feelings dwindle? To the same places the starlings fly in the spring? Or is it as Ellinor says: love doesn't exist. It's only a euphemism. That's the horrible reality of most marriages. And that's why one of our first acts as a married couple will be to file for a divorce.'

MELANCHOLY

The Grand Art Theft in San Nicola

When his wife called from Paris, Adriano was sitting at a table in the dinette of their San Nicola home sipping Pernod and examining Dürer's *Melencolia 1*. The only light was a lamp pointing at the framed copy of the engraving hanging on the wall in front of him. The tenebrous depths of the rest of the room intensified his pleasant isolation from the world.

When in the darkness a shutter banged, he jumped slightly. The familiar north wind had begun pounding against windows and doors, its blasts soon shaking the whole house. He turned his eyes away from Dürer to listen to the ferocious *tramontana* wind that he loved, nodded approvingly and took a distracted sip from a tall glass of Pernod. From time to time he shifted his eyes from the engraving to contemplate his own shadowy reflection in the wall mirror hanging alongside the framed picture—gaunt face, pale forehead, lower lip projected, chicken neck, long hair and full beard, one slim arm lying stretched across the table. He thought he resembled an old portrait molded by time that had left a permanent melancholy in his eyes, in his reflection shiny like the eyes of the sad woman in the engraving.

Adriano imagined that he was inside the art he was studying, inside the polyhedron, inside the sadness of the despondent woman with light eyes and the look of one mourning for the death of an angel. Yet even from his dreamy conceptual position inside the engraving, he still found the art psychologically disturbing.

Maybe it was a coincidence he thought that precisely at the moment he felt he was about to make some sense of one of the most puzzling works of art in existence, his art dealer wife telephoned from Paris to recite more of her existential fabrications ... a reflection on the very art she profited from. The ring blasted him out of Dürer's tumultuous sixteenth century atmosphere of the melancholy woman and the countless beings and objects scattered around her.

As ever more frequently, Margot was hysterical. Their Paris apartment had been ransacked … in broad daylight. And the idiotic concierge didn't see a thing. 'Thank God I wasn't there,' she yelled. 'The burglars took everything. Your computer. Our Bose radio stuff … and the Dürer engraving. Oh, I don't yet know what all. We should call a condominium meeting and fire that spineless woman who never sees anyone come or go as she's supposed to. I still think she's receiving male clients in the backroom of her loge ... she's … that bitch … she's'….

'No problem, Margot,' he reassured her. 'It's all insured, *Tesoro.* Just call the agent. His number is in the file. And please forget the concierge. She has to have some additional income … considering her miserable salary.'

'Alors, en tout cas, I can't possibly return to Rome tomorrow as planned. Unless, uh, well, I'll call the agent and maybe fly out in the afternoon. Got to report it to the police first and then … and see …'

'And see to things,' Adriano finished the sentence for her in the same dismissive way she always did. 'Of course you do, *Tesoro.'*

'Alors, à la prochaine, Cheri,' Margot said, audibly relieved by his understanding.

'Once the love of my life,' he mused, 'Margot is the personification of an effrontery to human intelligence.' Adriano smiled painfully, but with the satisfaction of a clever man when he uncovers his wife's betrayal. Then, automatically, he corrected himself aloud: 'I AM A LYING SON OF A BITCH … for she still is the love of my life.'

It happened every time. Every time she went to Paris some disaster befell her and their pampered apartment overlooking Les Invalides and Napoleon's cannons. Misadventures that happened only to her ... if they even happened. It's her theatrical style of life, Adriano knew. The way *she* desires things to be become for her reality. Her cosmic world view.

Outside, the wind blew. Shutters banged. The whole house shuddered. Pensively he took a long drink of Pernod, then held the glass to the lamp and contemplated the cloudy and milky color it had assumed when he added water.

Actually he knew what was going on in Paris. She knew he knew and he knew she knew. Their relationship had become a charade that exhausted them both just to keep alive a spark of what once was. Though he was sick and tired of living so much alone in the Rome suburb while she did whatever she did in Paris, at times he still felt that tickle of desire for her. Especially now, after her phone call and the dream image of her of the night before. Of their spring meeting on Via del Corso seven years ago, she in her shortest miniskirt, in Rome researching the artist Masaccio for her dissertation and he the up-and- coming journalist … and three hours later they in bed in a Piazza del Pantheon hotel.

'That is,' he reminded himself, 'the dream returned this morning at two a.m.' Tired of work, tired of googling wildly, he'd thrown himself on the bed, stared at the ceiling, listened a bit to Brahms on the boom box, when in the first phase of falling asleep, in a sort of trance, more imagination than the dream he kept having, he again saw themselves as newlyweds, barely in their twenties, hand in hand on the steps of the Metropolitan Museum that Margot the arts graduate had so wanted to see. In the great entrance hall—now deep in the dream—just next to the ticket counters hung a row of copies of Melencolia 1. He counted ten copies ... maybe more. 'But they're not alike,' she cried. People gathered around. The ticket seller wanted to be paid if Margot even looked at the prints. 'Each one's different. Fakes, Adriano. They're all fakes. Where can we see a real Melencolia 1? There are only six in the world. But not here. Where oh where can we see one? Just one. Where?' He woke in a sweat, gasping for air. He didn't know where they could see a real one either.

Yet, he told himself, he had other options. He didn't have to play the eternal fool waiting for her. There were alternatives to Margot. He was not obligated to live alone, nor did his friend Raffaella have to live alone, either. She was there for him, only a few hundred meters away in San Nicola. He cared for her, too. Yes, he would go over to Raffaella's place tomorrow morning. She had lots of comfort and solace to share. But what held him to crazy Margot? Or was it that one thing in her? Her madness! He knew. And her ever present innocence about the most obvious situations which prompted her childlike fibs. Yes, it was that, too. The quality, Adriano believed, without which no person was whole.

A gust of wind again shook the house.

He took another drink of the milky Pernod.

Adriano grimaced in a sudden sensation of Schadenfreude for Margot's situation. Well, let her work things out. Come and go as she likes! The fundamental problem, he concluded as many times before, was that Margot was a pathological liar. From the start her attempts to be many persons in one had misled them both. The problem with Margot was Margot. A month ago he'd brought back to Rome the Bose audio set, his Paris computer, as well as her framed copy of Melencolia 1 that he was now trying to interpret for his weekly magazine column. And she hadn't even noticed the absence of her beloved masterpiece. Her non-presence at the apartment at Les Invalides was so conspicuous. Now, however, his fascination with this small engraving so packed with symbols—weighing scales, a 4x4 magic number square, a sad putto, a sleeping dog, a hand saw—drew him back to the gaze of the unhappy woman staring at the block of wood in the shape of a polyhedron. Dürer's woman is sitting with her chin in her hand, her arm propped on a knee, her eyes sharp but despondent which again reminded him of Margot. She has angel's wings. And with a ladder standing behind her reaching toward heaven. She is sitting there as people with afflicted minds do, people carried away by absurdities. But that strange block of polished wood thwarts her desire to climb the ladder to heaven. The three dimensional polyhedron with sharp edges and corners and flat face that stares back at her … stared at Adriano as well.

The unhappy woman's melancholy shined forth: if the great artist that was Dürer put it in this engraving it must be significant. Abruptly, Adriano saw *it* again. He jumped to his feet and leaned closer to the picture and all at once the face of the polyhedron looking straight at him seemed transformed. The geometric face had metamorphosed into the face of many-sided, egocentric, closed-on-herself Margot ... the same gleam in her eyes as in Dürer's melancholy woman, the same sensuous resistance of her body, her hair free and uncontrolled.

In recent times Adriano had begun to see more clearly into the dark side of his wife, the shadow in her that wouldn't let her go … or that she wouldn't let go. He didn't know which. But it was there. He knew it was always there, the shadow. During the first two or three years of their togetherness he'd been only vaguely aware of that obscure side of her. But as time passed her dark side had ploughed its way forward, emerged, and now seemed to dominate both their lives. Moreover, the shadow had tried—with some success, he admitted—to suck him into its orbit.

Although Margot's shadow looked out at him from the polyhedron, in no way whatsoever could he link Margot's real life image to the melancholic woman inside the artistic enigma. Most certainly Margot was not Dürer's unhappy winged angel. His Margot was not an angel. Nor was she depressed. So why did he see her there? Had hc misread his Margot? Or Dürer?

And there was also that number 1 to confuse matters: Melencolia 1. Many interpretations of its meaning existed: number one of a series of engravings, the first of three types of melancholy, the first of the four temperaments, And the one Adriano had settled on, the number 1 stands for *nigredo*, the first stage of the alchemical process, the blackness that alchemists considered the first step on the pathway to the *philosophers' stone*—the most sought after goal in alchemy in Dürer's times—the legendary substance that turns base metals into gold, the elixir of life, perfection, immortality, and heavenly bliss. And Dürer included the ladder to get there.

It happened that in that period Adriano was reading the psychoanalyst Mario Trevi's book, *Controlled Invasions*, struck by the analyst's words that not everyone who suffers is necessarily depressed. 'Like Job,' the Jungian wrote. 'In all his suffering, Job was not depressed; he was unhappy, yes, but not depressed. He was unhappy because he felt abandoned; despite wife and friends, he felt alone.' And Job, the writer noted, became wise and lived unhappily to an old age. Trevi reminded Adriano of Dostoevsky who wrote in *Crime and Punishment* that pain and suffering are inevitable for a large intelligence and a deep heart and that great men must have great sadness on earth. Now Adriano was both depressed *and* unhappy. And his Margot said the same of him as did Job's wife: Adriano was sad without reason; he enjoyed success in his work, was praised in the intellectual world and had a beautiful French wife. Yet one question in particular plagued Adriano and it concerned Dürer's work, the primary reason he'd carried the engraving to Rome: Can melancholy be linked to creativity? Some art historians think so. For Adriano, too, the light eyes of Dürer's female figure reflected the value of artistic creativity. But then he concluded that if most creative people experience inexplicable melancholy, that doesn't mean that every person who experiences melancholy is creative. Adriano's fear was that he belonged to the latter.

'That must be why I hold onto concrete things. The things of life that offer salvation.' He looked around him. The unused computer from their Invalides apartment. The photograph of their kitten that had vanished. A black and white photo of a beggar in the Santa Novella station in Florence. A Dutch-Spanish dictionary. A boom box he'd taken with him on a trek in the Alps when he was eighteen. An African face mask he'd acquired in Mali.

'Some of my things vanish,' he mused. 'But other objects remain. Perhaps destined to remain ... so that I can pass them down to my heirs. I hold onto those things, the objects whose destiny though different from mine are also me.' Yet he thought it's paradoxical that while I crave for the old things of the *normal,* I may submit to a new-normal that could permanently deny me any chance of ever returning to the old-normal I long for.

Again reviewing the things around him, Adriano concluded that *foreign* agents, agents outside our control, agents with their own vested interests—politicians, media, businessmen—construct our reality, much as a film-maker makes a movie or a writer constructs a book or as an artist designs an engraving. They guide our gaze in certain directions and not others. What we think of as "the real world", the "normal" world, is almost entirely manufactured for us. Clearly our attention is the plaything of others. That "real world", as it is presented to us, is

On the path of love we are neither the masters nor the owners of our lives. We are only a brush in the hand of the Master Painter. (Rumi)

merely a set of political, economic and social priorities that have been devised for us.

Turning back to the engraving he jerked himself out of his contemplations and realized that despite the stillness in the woman's melancholy, total chaos reigned in the scene just as it did in his own scene. In the darkness behind him the wind raged. Shutters slammed. The house shook. A glance in the Mexican mirror reflected his own blanched eyes. And again his restless gaze stopped on the mysterious light source illuminating the whole engraving now in movement, especially the melancholy woman's gleaming eyes. Then, as each time, he zeroed in on the banner born by a bat-like creature and spelled aloud the word Dürer had inscribed on the banner: 'M e l e n c o l i a', followed by that enigmatic number 1.

MARGOT

Margot counted the bronze cannons aligned along the moat in front of Les Invalides. 'Twenty!' she exclaimed. 'The same as last time.' The cannons had fascinated her since she heard them fired as a greeting to the new President of her country. And she'd studied the history of the cannons positioned practically under her front windows: sixteen captured from the Ottomans, three Chinese, one from Indochina, most of them bearing the inscription *ultima ratio regum*, the last argument of the kings.

She shrugged, turned away from the window facing the Esplanade and began another inspection of the third-floor apartment that she loved passionately. If only Adriano would agree to living here! Their problems would be resolved. He could forget that silly Raffaella affair and she wouldn't need arrogant Lucien anymore.

"*Quel bordel* we've created in our lives," she muttered just as Lucien appeared from the bedroom, buttoning primly his perfect jacket, which somehow irritated her more than she was at herself for her weakness of character.

'Bonjour, Lucien,' she said sarcastically.

'Bonjour, Margot, bonjour', the tall, good-looking man said joyously.

'And au revoir until the next time,' she added, the first realistic words she'd spoken to him that morning. 'You know, Lucien, I don't love you any more than Adriano loves that Italian woman.'

'So why continue?'

'You know why,' she admitted. 'You know my … uh, you know me well.' Too well, she thought.

For Margot, sex was the problem. She didn't even like perfectly dressed Lucien or his snobbish friends. But he did introduce her to his rich friends who became her clients. Sloppy and careless Adriano couldn't care less about his dress and made his best friends among plumbers and electricians and carpenters. She loved that in him. Their common problem was that Adriano needed "creativity" more than he did sex. For him, she knew, *his* Raffaella was merely a sounding board for his mad ideas.

A normal life together here at Les Invalides would bring some balance into their abnormal relationship. For she loved Adriano and she was sure he loved her. They had a past together. They had common goals. Yet normality was not the issue either. The real issue was that after their seven years together she still didn't know if he was mentally deranged or if he just chose to be … living as he did in his own fixations.

Lucien put on his dark blue cap in his self-satisfied manner, opened the door, turned, and said: 'By the way, where is that Dürer engraving that hung there next to window so long? A friend told me it was quite valuable and that he himself would buy it for 500,000 euros.'

'Insane! A half million for the copy of a print I bought from a *bouquiniste* near the Pont Neuf for fifty euros. And now you tell me it's real! Do you really think so, Lucien? I bought that one simply because I like it … and even had it framed. Do you think it's really worth … why, of course if it's an artist's copy it's worth many millions. Even a copy of one of the handful of prints the artist made is worth a lot more than that half million. And I thought it only had sentimental value. Now some fucking burglar has it and doesn't even know what he has in his hands … he probably took it only because it's framed.'

She remembered that the Metropolitan once had hundreds of copies of Dürer's *Melencolia 1*. Copies of other copies of copies that is.

Museum store stuff. But the number of real copies in the world seemed reduced to the ten of Adriano's dreams or more likely to zero. 'Oh, if they would all vanish except mine. As the last one extant it would truly be worth millions. Why, the world's great museums would all bid for it. Still, authentication is always a problem.'

She knew that impressions of the print change as the printing plate is repeatedly sent through the press. Adriano had suggested that Dürer's printing plate wore down and impressions just got lighter and lighter until the cutting no longer existed. Still, no one knows how many impressions Dürer was able to make. It was true that in her copy—a copy of a copy of a copy of some museum copy, she'd always believed—there was a strong horizontal scratch on the saw lying in the foreground under the sad woman's feet, a mark in the printing plate itself that occurred later in the printing. She wondered if that scratch gave her copy some legitimacy.

'Neither in heaven nor on Earth,' Adriano had said poetically. Margot loved him for that quality, too. But that familiar scratch now seemed like proof that this could be a genuine copy of a master print; that son-of-a-bitch Lucien's information made sense.

ADRIANO

Two a.m. No pleasant thoughts to soothe his seething mind occurred. No Metropolitan Museum memories returned. No trips this year to the Cinque Terre where he always found peace and inspiration. Melencolia 1 kept bobbing to the surface. Might as well make my own magic square, he thought. A 4x4 like Dürer's. If he could do it so easily I should be able to figure it out with time. Try number 25 as the goal. Row one horizontal: 7-5-9-4=25. First vertical column 7-6-8-4=25, then the rest. But the numbers of the diagonals are another story. Palindromes of words you can read from either direction are simple in comparison. Ah, those diabolical diagonals! Now how did he do it? Well, first of all, Dürer was a genius. Or he hired a numerical genius to plot it for him. But no. A cheap solution like that was for the herd. His was an age when a genius was a giant. They didn't go for specialists who did only one thing. No stooping to shortcuts. No gaslighting the public. No false deeds. Anyway, the rows and columns are regular. A piece of cake. Got to work on the diagonals. They'll get you every time.

'So what the fuck'—he said aloud in English, imitating his rough-speaking wife who loved that international phrase—'what the fuck can I do with our framed Melencolia 1?' First: a burglar allegedly stole it. Second: if she can prove it has value, there will be a settlement. Third: Nah, she can't prove it. No one can. Authentication of art work is complex. Big money moves that world. And I don't believe it's worth much anyway. It's just a copy like those we saw at the Metropolitan that time. *Jamais de la vie* a half million. And who cares? We've got enough. It's only money. Better to get our lives in order.

In any case, Signor Dürer, your puzzling work can't stay here. You don't know my Margot. And you never know with her. She comes home tomorrow still thinking the burglar in Paris stole it and she reported the theft of a valuable artwork to the insurance agent. So I can't leave it here on the wall … even if the engraving is worth no more than the price of its frame. So for now I'll stash it away and someday it can resurface. Willy-nilly, as she likes to say.

That night an image of Margot walking into their house in San Nicola flashed across his eyes. She stops in confusion, then explodes in a fury at the sight of the engraving hanging next to the magical Mexican mirror, Adriano leapt from the bed and to his surprise found that he was still fully dressed. It was nearly three a.m.

A gust of tramontana again shook the house.

He ran down the stairs barefoot, downed a half glass of Pernod straight, unhung Dürer's masterpiece, and stopped to contemplate his shadowy self in the cracked mirror grimacing back at him. Raffaella was in for a surprise: she was about to become the keeper of a copy of a copy of a copy of the legendary Melencolia 1.

Visions

My visual field is truly strange. Everything is blurred. Everything limited. Narrow. It's bizarre. And I don't know when or how it came about. Those shapeless and white, green and blue phantoms fluttering down that tunnel. My tunnel. A tunnel that can only lead to another tunnel. Dancing phantoms. Strange too, those dark dancers. Surely as rare a vision as the Drucina Championi butterfly at the top of the volcano Atatenango. Now that is a crazy recollection in a moment like this. At 3796 meters protruding out of Guatemalan earth butterflies fluttering and dancing in the cold breeze. They too distorted phantasmal figures. There for only an instant before vanishing in a flash into the fire of red hot lava. It's all so grotesque. Again, I try to blink. Again, in vain. My eyes are as fixed as the absurd theater of white and green and blue contortionists fluttering into and fading out of my tunnel. If they would only stop their jerking around like Italian marionettes so that I can decipher this ridiculous situation. But wait! What was that? Patience! It will return. A deformed red shape is drawing near. Now it's hovering. Is it searching for my ghosts? Is it Death? That balloon figure with bulging eyes is leaning toward me. It's jabbering something, maybe about me to some other form somewhere outside my visual realm. I don't get a word. Well, let them babble. I will ignore them and think about Dunya. They can decide everything. It all matters so little now. In my fixed state I just have to stay focused on the few certainties passing through my still perceptive mind. Elimination of fantasies and impossible variations is, however, hardly consoling progress. My distant past is the complex element. How to deal with that past is the question. Once it arrived in the guise of the present, dallied a short time, and was gone. Piff! Gone. Flying on the Caribbean winds. The only certainty is still Dunya … my world, Dunya. Her name is as fixed as a name inscribed on a gravestone in the Père-Lachaise city of the dead. Since we were children she has been the one certainty on which I could count. Maybe she, too, is somewhere in the shadows lying outside of my visual tunnel. If so, she could step forward and explain what this is all about? This thing in me. And the phantoms. The great red dot. This paralyzing tunnel I'm in. Such peculiar visions. The word *massive* hangs in the thickening white air. It's like being the main character in a *pesadilla*. A pantomime in a nightmare. Magical happenings. A whisper. Do I exist? Am I anything at all? Have I ever been anything? Or, or, or, am I, maybe, already, dead?

If it were not for the remembrances! Or do the dead remember after all? Now I can try. I have only time anyway. Like when Dunya left, I had nothing but time left. That was when the turmoil began. She left home, left Santiago, left me behind. Abruptly she left for Europe. Only *there* could she "make it". Make her career. In the tunnel I can see all my yesterdays. Dim and distorted … maybe unreal. Real was that Dunya had to dance. Since she was a child she was a ballerina. She couldn't not dance. What could Santiago de Cuba offer the ballerina Dunya Betancourt? Nothing. Nothing at all. Havana offered little. Mexico, only the allure and the unknown. So it was to Europe. To Europe. And someday soon I had to follow. Oh, I remember. Was memory my undoing? My greatest regret? Or is my real regret not missing the other present? The one always around me? The new in that past? Missing the revolution? Yes, the revolution. And my part in it. In this mysterious present in which our brief but myriad past keeps marching across and through, marching, marching through the tunnel of my mind's eyes.

Do the white and green and blue phantoms not see it, too? Don't they see my memories marching? My unswerving eyes miss nothing, not the smallest detail do my eyes miss. They miss nothing within this narrow field of vision that is mine. The marching past, a potential past, a cortege headed by Dunya. Like Raskolnikov's Dunya, compassionate Dunya. Criminal the one; compassionate the other.

To think that I was only twenty when I too left. Now I am … I am … How old am I? Peculiar, my age escapes my memory. Memory is truly a rover. Escapes time. But it's still alive. Still alive. But not in my time. Time is truant, too. Does time not live? Strange feeling, not knowing your age. Like not knowing your name. Anti-revolutionary convictions had no role in my departure. I had no such convictions. Not me. I, Rafael, was a believer. In Dunya. In the revolution. Had my family's once vast agricultural lands not been confiscated by the corrupt Havana government for Yankee mafia companies. Seen in that light my departure was heroic. In order to play the hero in Dunya's eyes … and to gain the esteem of my father who advised me that if I truly loved Dunya, I had to fight for her. Go to Paris. Get a university degree there, find Dunya, bring her back home, join the revolution and restore our estate. Restore the sugarcane fields.

Again in the Latin American student dormitory in Paris I was torn between supporters of the revolution and anti-Fidelistas. My bravado self had wanted to be with Fidel and Raul on board the *Granma* arriving from Mexico … Rafael de la Costa, national hero. How I wanted to be loved. And celebrated. No moping around the dormitory in Paris, a blanket around my shoulders in the winter and singing mournful exile songs. But internally I did sing, *Cuando salì de Cuba* … . I was not a refugee. Nor an exile. I was a revolutionary. Still, I had to have Dunya like before. The clamorous clash of desires. I remember. Sometimes, during Parisian winter nights, I liked to imagine myself leading an attack through the tight serried ranges and forbidding valleys of the guerrilla territory in the Sierra Maestra … while Dunya waited for me down in Santiago. Was her love strong enough? The spectacular vistas over the plains below with the sugarcane fields and the *macheteros* in tattered linens and straw sombreros slashing left and right with their blunt-nosed machetes. All these memories: the familiar smells, the heat of the sun's blinding rays, the warm wind caressing my face, a decades old Chrysler impervious to the mountainous terrain passing the single file of ragged revolutionaries. Upwards, ever upwards, Cuba's highest peaks within fingertip distance. All these heights and volcanoes and rare *mariposas*. And as light fades in the mountains the warm lights of Santiago de Cuba beckon in the distance below where Dunya waits. A rose radiance colors the mountains and sunlight paints Santiago's rooftops fiery red. Oh, the splendor, the magnificence of memories.

And for this moment, I can see the red roofs, I feel my breathing accelerate and the fever rise and … and I regret leaving Cuba. All Cubans think that way. But that I have to keep secret from the dancing white and the green and the blue phantoms in the tunnel.

In the reality of school days in Santiago I really knew I would've hated tramping around the mountains with the revolutionary fighters. I would see the vermillion of Santiago rooftops another time … from another perspective. Besides, most of those fighters would probably die there. And I didn't want to die; I wanted to live my life to the fullest even though Dunya had mocked me. Always she'd mocked me … that I just wanted to *be* a hero … not *become* one. She said I saw life only in the present in which I didn't have to *become* anything, while only slowly, slowly the future arrived, always in the present. I could never be a revolutionary, she said. They themselves bring about change and build a new future. Sometimes I hated her for that; and I never acknowledged that she was right. Such clear insight into myself however underpins my unspoken perceptions of the overall correctness of my existential choices. Awareness of the former lucidity of my thought was elating, even in this moment sparkling in the tight, dimly illuminated tunnel of this channel vision.

Bad things had been going on back there on Cuba's beaches when you might face a Russian T-34 tank. Or even in Santiago too. In the whole Southeast. In Cuba in general. And I'd been caught up in it all. Yet I didn't go to Playa Giròn. I'd just wanted to be out of it all. On the one hand, I'd wanted to escape from the provinces where I'd been a prisoner since birth. But escape meant departure. And exile, and betrayal. Bitter images of those millions of *gusanos de Miami*, the worms, drinking *café escaso* on Collins Avenue and Flagler Street and Little Havana. Oh, I celebrated. Like a victorious militia man I rejoiced at the victory over the Gringos. The CIA army of *gusanos*s smashed. Oh, the elation. The celebrations. Captured invaders: 100 former plantation owners, 67 former landlords, 35 former factory owners, 112 businessmen, 194 ex-Batista soldiers. Should I have celebrated the executions, too? I didn't know if I had the right. Yet, I am a real Cuban, not a water-wading *gusano* in the Pigs Bay.

The story was the same at the Sorbonne: I didn't want to study and commit myself to the task of *becoming* a famous architect. But it was easy to acknowledge to those silly academic advisers that I would like to *be* one. A conceptual architect. Me, Rafael.

Dunya was right. Dunya always knew. Dunya had always been right. Now where is she? She was part of it all. Of this life. Though absent from my vision in this bizarre situation, she must be there in the impenetrable shadows, near but distant from this condition of living only in my eyes. Yes, Dunya had always known that what I really wanted was freedom ... freedom from restraints and limits.

It was the nature of things. Strange nature, the Cuban. How easily the *gusanos* betrayed. Cuban traitors all. This tunnel I live in is driving me crazy. What's really going on?

From the time Dunya got her first soloist job in the Stuttgart Ballet, I *was* her manager. In Germany. I didn't go back to Cuba when Castro's revolutionaries finally crushed the old and brought in the new. Neither *gusano* nor hero, I stayed in Europe. Found Dunya and devoted myself to our career. Oh, yes, our career! Above all, my career. Is that where I am now? Is this Germany?

Dunya and her *amor sinfin! Amor eterno.* She'd been my life. Always. From the moment of her flight to Europe my existence in Santiago turned black. Onyx black. Her *amor eterno* for me wasted away like the thousands of acres of our estate.

Where oh where am I? Havana? Paris? Germany? Our estate back there just dwindled away. Taxed out of existence. The old trick: hyper taxation; rapid confiscation. By Batista and his Gringos. They'd always hated Santiago. Hated the whole Oriente of Cuba. Stole our sugar cane, stole our coffee beans, and let other crops die.

But I couldn't live without her, without what Dunya had given me since we were still nearly children. Only to me. the snob, as she called me when I derided our provincial roots. My obsession with her drove us both crazy.

The once most elegant *finca* in eastern Cuba was going to ruins, the staff reduced to the cook-chauffeur and the gardener do-it-all. Padre had capitulated. Surrendered in face of the fiscal machine in corrupt Havana. Twelve long hours away. Hours as hard as the climb to the top of Acatenango Volcano. And still not far enough away for the old man who refused to move to the Capital as most other landholders of the Southeast had done. Sitting in his study where he lived his life of ex-landowner, scribbling useless orders and pointless instructions for non-existent employees like a kulak waiting for the knock on the door in '32. Or reading dreamy histories of Old Cuba, and waiting to be served his favorite mouth-pinching constipation-exasperating fried green plantains, the once vigorous land owner, a tall and handsome man suddenly came to seem older than he was. I, his only son, was surprised when I realized the old man in the book-lined study was only fifty-two.

The servants whispered to me, Rafael. Every day they whispered warnings. 'He's ageing too fast. He can't live on bananas ... and he can't shit. Plantains are turning him inside out.' As if a son could make things right. The son had no voice. Anyway, they were crazy in Havana to destroy the provinces which fed them.

Dunya gone, my father wasting together with our former lives, at one point I had faced the dilemma: flee to Mexico … with Dunya. And there join that mad man Fidel and his brother Raul. To change things and be a hero. Or rather, go to Europe with Dunya.

But after her departure there was no choice. No alternatives. I had to abandon my father, the *finca*, the Revolution and go to Paris in search of my Dunya.

Dunya? How to explain her. Even her name rang crazy. Her father had read *Crime and Punishment* to her mother during her pregnancy and both parents had loved the name, Dunya. As I did. I read the book, too … just to know. Raskolnikov's sister, Dunya, was compassionate, while Dostoevsky's protagonist, like me, was arrogant and egotistical. Dunya and I, Rafael, loved each other as did Raskolnikov and Dostoevsky's Dunya: she selflessly; I possessively. We grew up together. We learned sex together while we were children in the capital of the East. Life was meaningless without her.

Dunya was compassionate but not selfless; she chose to escape to make her own life. "I have to have more than the Cuban provinces," she said. "My talent merits the fame and glory that await me over there." Mexico was no solution. She would leave me for Europe and for the dance. Our love life was not her first priority, while I, the only son, was obligated to see things through to the end.

"Padre, you do realize they've taken most of our land and we're reduced to this country house, three riding horses, a few cows and a vegetable garden much of which those crazy Cuban crows eat. Havana and Batista stole the rest."

"But the Yankees paid us well, *hijo*!"

"Bah! Money in the bank! In which currency? Pesos? And if it all collapses? What will your millions of pesos be worth then?"

"Son, don't think like a landowner! Times are changing."

"Papà, I mean another kind of change. There are people over in Mexico, Cubans who want to change things much, much faster. This little we have left is not going to last forever. You know them, the Castros. Why not give them a hand now? I read that even the Chicago mafia diversified its investments. The Castros get some too. You can do the same."

"Nothing lasts forever, *hijo*. We get old and we die. But meanwhile we have to get you into the university in France so that whatever happens you can take care of yourself. We've got money to spend! I've got money in Mexico and some in Europe, too. I was always thinking ahead."

"Okay, okay. But you have to think about Mamà and yourself. If the revolution comes here you might lose the little you have left here in Santiago and your bank accounts in Havana, too."

Like Dunya's parents, my father had good reason to fear that loud knock on the door late at night. The "Santiago crowd" they were called. Castro supporters. Santiago itself was suspect. Everybody there preparing for the Castros' return to make their revolution. There was little difference between Batista's police and the Tonton Macoute, the zombies, we could nearly see across the straits separating us from Haiti. On a good day you could imagine you see the island of evil. In reality, Santiago's hate for Havana was not so much for political reasons. Both fathers hated the Batista bureaucracy in Havana as much as the American mafia loved it. And Havana tolerated no disobedience in the provinces. Pay the *protection* or perish.

Still, Santiago fathers, Havana fathers, fathers in the provinces knew no more than did Havana politicos about what their children's generation was thinking. What we and the Castros were thinking.

Dunya and I were children when our bond was sealed. In Santiago de Cuba. Fourteen, fifteen, sixteen, seventeen years old. She danced in her studio. No parental controls for compassionate, passionate, unlimited Dunya. I brushed her hair and squeezed her feet when she had her first periods, there in Santiago de Cuba. Oh, how I brushed her long hair. How she danced in her studio-love nest. Our story passes slowly or maybe fast before me now and I keep wondering if the white and green and blue figures saw it when we made children's love in Dunya's bed in her studio in Santiago.

Ours is a story, the story I love most. Our Santiago story. Reliving it makes it live now in this fixed state of white and green and blue confusion and the dark shadows filled with both promise and threat. The kisses, the fumbling, the touching of our secret parts in the tropical evenings in the shadows in her studio in Cuba. Our love scents filled the air. The air of Oriente Province, where the light breeze comes in from the sea every passing day.

The two children, clearly Dunya and I, now march across my unmoving, unclosable eyes and then their figures vanish into the shadows. My real self reaches for her. And for the first time I know: it has always been *my* story more than *ours*. Now it is over. I belong to this *massive* whatever it is that has overcome me. Now I just wish one of those deformed phantoms would step out of the tunnel and close my eyes for me. Once and for all.

JUAN FRANCISCO GETS A HANDLE ON LIFE

Maliciously he turned up the volume of the boom box blasting Mexican country music into the room. Anything to shake her from the bed and to dampen the roar of the intense morning traffic on the steep cobblestone street just outside the ground level window. After a long mental search for a subject he knew offended and irritated her most, Juan Francisco looked up from his easel and scowled at her curled form in the narrow bed a few steps away.

"You simply don't have any idea what the real world is," he said. "You're thirty years old, *verdad*? But you're still the spoiled rich girl from Mexico City-Las Lomas ... still dependent on your doting father."

When he saw her twitch, he smiled to himself and let his last words sink in before continuing, louder than before.

"When are you going to grow up, for Chrissakes. You don't even know why you're here, right? If you know, tell me: *Why are you here*? And just don't mention the word love, pleasseee. So why? Tell me why. The truth is—you know what the truth is?—you don't want to grow up. You know what you should do, *niña bien*? You should go back home and live your life with Papá and the rest of your class."

Marisa squirmed and wriggled at his words pouring down on her. It was that 'rest of your class' that got to her. He said class though actually they were his origins too even though he shouted to the winds that he'd rejected that 'disgusting bourgeois class'. Still, above all, she hated his epithet, *niña bien*, the spoiled rich girl.

Two lamps illuminated the big canvas he was working on. The gas stove in the corner near the window burned red, making the long narrow room with lime-washed walls and high ceilings cozy. But Juan Francisco, Johnny, her Juan, was out of tune, out of tune with the setting, out of tune with life. And furthermore, despite his two sweaters and thick wool scarf, she saw he was freezing. The cold mornings were unbearable for him standing immobile in front of the easel.

"You don't like me, do you?" he shot at her covered form, and theatrically threw his brush on the tile floor. "You've never liked me. God knows why you put up with me. You just have to have a man, *verdad*? And you don't want to be the *niña bien*, do you? But it's in your blood."

From an initial trickle his words had become a stream, then a torrent.

Marisa snuggled deeper under the covers.

"You are what you are and you'll always be that, *niña bien.* Just that. You can't escape it. You can live with an artist, you can sleep around all you want, you can smoke and drink, you can have your own apartment and vacation in La Jolla, but you'll always be Papá's little girl—a product of Las Lomas, Mexico City. Away from there, you're lost. You think you're immune to the problems that face everyone else but no, dearest little girl, you don't even know what the real world is about. You …"

Marisa covered her ears. Will he never stop? As if I were responsible for where I was born. Real life! As if he knew what it is. He talks and talks. Unceasingly he talks, talks, talks. Relentlessly. He has to say everything possible on every subject. He talks in crowds. He talks to himself, to his paintings, to the mirror, but most of all to me. I'm his sounding board. Egocentric tyrant.… But he's right. What am I doing here? I don't need him. If I were just not afraid he'd die without me! Or go completely insane. I'll leave him anyway. I will. Most certainly I'm going to quit. Maybe today. I've said it so many times. It's unbearable. He makes love to me in the evenings and hangs onto my breasts all night and wakes me every few hours to talk more. Or he gets up to turn on the stove. Or to feed the cat … and to talk to me. I'll leave him. I will.

Juan Francisco Alvarez was considered the best painter in the town. The town didn't deserve him, he himself said. So superior was his work to that of the hundreds of painters in San Miguel that he thought of his hill overlooking the town as Parnassus. He was here because of his mother, he said. Not because of some extreme filial attachment but because she had this big house and she needed his financial support. Anyway, he'd been at loose ends in Mexico City after Gertrude left, after his bouts with alcohol, cocaine … and that bad marriage.

Thank God his small paintings sold well in the restaurants and minor galleries here as they once had in Mexico City—the wretched things he used to throw out the windows in a drunken rage. He felt like burning it all. His shrink Fiedler said it was the typical case of the creator who fears his own greatness.

But those paintings are not the real Juan Francisco Alvarez. My real art is here in the back room of my studio. Or still in my head.

He stared toward Marisa, aware of his hatred of his dependence on her—on the assurance a woman brings. His mother was another thing. Her life, *pobrecita*, poor thing, revolved around him. She got up in the mornings to have her Johnny's coffee ready. She set her watch by him. That is, she had until a few months ago when she shattered his new life. For no acceptable reason she took a lover. She brought her lover into the house. Esteban López was up there now. Esteban, the usurper. Screwing his mother. Distracting his mother from her son. What ingratitude! What neglect! What maternal wantonness!

It was already nine, maybe ten o'clock, and he hadn't yet had his coffee. Again he frowned at Marisa. Why wasn't she up? Up and playing her proper role of buffer between him and the upstairs couple, his mother Elizabeta and Esteban.

He turned and looked in the big mirror he used for self-portraits … and also his favorite bed games. He smiled to himself, adjusted his scarf and ran his hand through receding but still dark hair that he wore straight back. Thick sensuous lips turned outwards revealed his very white teeth marred by two brown ones in the upper center. He closed his mouth. He was pleased when people spoke of his Roman nose, strong and expressive. He liked his smooth wrinkleless face that when he wasn't talking was apparently calm and reflective; yet he and everyone else knew it concealed a stormy nature. Tall and slim, with a narrow waist, good shoulders and his mother's wide blue Swedish eyes, Juan Francisco knew he was a handsome man.

He turned his head to the left and right and admired his strong profile. "Thank God for Mother's Swedish blood running through my veins," he murmured.

He looked then at Marisa's reflection in the mirror. She had sat up in bed. He liked her naked breasts. And her tousled morning look. She was a sexy woman. She looked even more striking in the mirror. Not that she wasn't also beautiful. Like many Mexican women after thirty a little heavy but she was tall and dark, with big black eyes, creamy skin and hard protruding breasts. Her beauty was classical. Nonetheless, he knew he was right—Marisa Romero was the prototype of the *niña bien*. Poor thing! But she was right, too—it wasn't her fault that she was the product of an all-encompassing system. At least she was trying to break out. I have no right to treat her that way. But that's just the way I am.

"Would you please go upstairs and get the coffee," he said as gently as possible. "You know I can't work without it."

"Okay, okay, I'm going." Marisa slid her feet along the cold terra-cotta floor, stepped into woolen slippers, slipped on his robe and stood behind Juan Francisco. Instinctively she wrapped her arms around him from behind, raised the scarf, and kissed the back of his neck. Peeking around him she searched for his eyes in the mirror. Just as she expected, the wild look was there. It was going to be a bad day. He said she was spoiled—in reality everyone spoiled Johnny, as the family called Juan Francisco. Now with his big exhibition in France coming up in the fall, he was like a child. And since Esteban was up there in the main house, Elizabeta was no longer at his beck and call and most of the spoiling now fell to her.

The exhibition, the exhibition, that's all he talked about, day and night, night and day. The eccentric artist she had known in their first months together, thoughtful and romantic, had become a monster. The exhibition would make him rich and famous, he claimed. It would change their life style. It would make him independent of his mother's house—and him free of me, she thought.

He heard the studio door close and her muffled steps on the stone stairs outside. How could he explain that this exhibition had stopped time? In some of his lost moments when he shut out the world and retreated into himself, there was no mother, no sister either—his lost sister, Oh Gertrude, my one and only love, if you were only here! How could you leave me? No family left, no friends, no events. And nothing happened. No news, no changes, no additions to his life. The exhibition and fame lay in the uncertain future and Gertrude and love in the irretrievable past. Today nothing existed except Marisa's breasts during the night and the cursed paintings during the day.

Oh good God! Did he deserve this? The winter was winding down and he had to finish by August. He was in the thick of the battle, his hands bruised and battered, his studio filled with half-finished canvases, Marisa-Gertrude at night, his mother and Esteban in his guts, and his cat hungry. And no events.

Well, not exactly no events. Three days ago at the café where evenings he played chess, he'd come to blows with his adversary, an old friend, who was taking too much time for a move. He deserved it. And what a good feeling it was. It had been pent-up, that blow. Release. Fulfillment. Many times more rewarding than slapping Marisa. The startled look on Roberto's face when I backhanded him, catching him on his cheekbone. It was worth the drubbing he gave me, he thought, chuckling to himself in the mirror and rubbing his bruised forehead.

If Marisa were not such a prig! If she would only punish me. Father did. Gertrude did. If she only had the guts, the passion and violent nature, the necessary cruelty, if she only had the courage, our relationship could be complete. But no, she's what she is too. They all think I'm insane and they pamper me. How I need something else.

He suspected his mother spoke behind his back with his psychiatrist about his progress. Or lack of it. They'd never really cured him. What did they want to cure him of anyway? Of being a Mexican? They'd taught him how to live with his symptoms. They'd taught him to survive. But he coddled his hypochondria, his claustrophobia, his paranoia—they had names for everything—his occasional agoraphobia. He joked that he had so many manias that he was half Greek. He held his quirks close.

His therapist—a German, and a Freudian to boot—was supposed to be good at eliminating symptoms. He and the others agreed on the diagnosis: manic depression. He could recite their diagnoses. When he was on a high he did become violent. Fiedler told him it was at the moment he began reemerging from depression that he became aggressive.

"It's normal," Fiedler said.

When he was on a low he was so morose that people considered him a snob ... or a troglodyte. He didn't care which. As if being Mexican were either normal or abnormal. They were right, he was not at fault. As he soared upward, omniscient, again omnipotent, he'd beaten his wife, hit Marisa, screamed at his mother, destroyed his paintings, terrorized his friends. Manic-depressive! So hopeless. So final. Like having short fingers or big feet. Manic-depressive! The only proof they had was his symptoms, and he wasn't about to surrender them. He told the German that he didn't care, that we're all depressives anyway, and that besides he was on good terms with death.

"Like all Mexicans," was the most old Fiedler could come up with.

He grinned obliquely at Marisa when she appeared with a tray of big mugs of coffee and the sweet breakfast rolls he loved. "Is he up there?" he asked softly.

"Esteban is so thoughtful toward your mother—and us, too. He said to tell you good morning and that he would drop in later."

"That swine!"

She paused, aware that her next words would wreck him. "Uh, Juan Francisco, he said to tell you I wouldn't have to come up for coffee much longer. You'll soon be able to move upstairs, he said. They're going to move to his house in Guadalajara."

His hand extended to take a roll, Juan Francisco froze.

"The pig!" he whispered.

"The *Schweinhund*! *Cabrón*! *Hijo de la Chingada*." His voice rose with every epithet. "Take Mother to Guadalajara! He's out of his fucking mind. She would never leave this house anyway. What a monster! Marisa, amor," he whispered again, "doesn't he repel you?"

Juan Francisco knew Marisa liked the man's gallant manners—his little Latin courtesies, his superficiality. But she too should feel repulsion for his mother's lover, the lowest, the most powerful, endless, unrelenting repulsion. The same loathing and disgust he felt for Esteban and his fucking hand kissing and fucking compassionate words.

Unfortunately, he himself could muster only the shadow of the repulsion he used to be able to feel for everything. Now only rancor remained. Was it a sign of advancing age? Well, most human creatures were creeps anyway. Not worth his repulsion. Disgust is one thing, repulsion another. He no longer even turned away. Cynically, he accepted one and all. Except that *cabrón* Esteban who wanted to abduct his mother.

Ah, repulsion! How wonderful it once was. Like the repulsion you can feel for sewer rats. What a loss! A vacuum. Especially the repulsion he could once feel for this town, for its exiled people like himself, for its life style. Who knows how he'd lost his sense of repulsion along the way? Suddenly, from one day to the next, he'd come to feel that he was above it. That it no longer existed for him. He no longer even felt the former repulsion for his art.

"Is that not progress?" he once asked Fiedler. When the therapist just nodded and instead asked him to speak instead of the things that counted for him, he could say truthfully, "Well, I care for my sins. Besides my art, they're the only things that are mine alone—that and my loneliness ... that is me."

"I think it's wonderful for Elizabeta," Marisa said, "after her hard life. It's diverting. She's been alone so long. You just want her to live for you. Admit it."

"Diverting! I'm working eighteen hours a day, my world is dayless and nearly nightless, and you say it's diverting. Now she has no real goals in life. Just serving that conniving bastard. As if it were her duty!"

"You're the most egocentric person I've ever known."

"And you've known quite a few." Although he considered himself above jealousy, her past lovers threatened him. Today as always his dark terror was of remaining alone. In those years when he was abandoned in Mexico City, his life was reduced to two choices—he could either walk the streets alone, or he could paint alone. Oh, if Marisa would only erupt violently, cruelly and rise over him and punish him, she could perhaps then truly love him. And redeem him. Instead, she remained the *niña bien*—fixed, immobile, unresponsive to his needs.

"Sometimes you're horrid."

"You only know to go from man to man."

He knew he was being cruel. And dishonest. He knew that her promiscuity was in pure innocence. Naively, she believed that normal life outside Las Lomas was like that. That was not to say that she felt like the emancipated woman. Not at all. Her life was simplicity itself. Marisa just had no conception of moral restrictions. In a way he envied her—she was amoral like a child, a reflection of her entire class. If she was lost at thirty years of age, for her it was not a question of getting a grip on life. It was just about marrying some man. Above all, a rich man. There's only one kink in her bourgeois social armor—actually her redemption, Juan thought, grinning at her candor—she loves to fuck.

"You have remarkable insight into me," he admitted, again speaking softly. "You're right about separation. I could never bear it. As a boy I always cried when someone left. Yet separation is my life." He wanted to continue but he was not about to reveal the urgency of his need of her nocturnal breasts to bring him closer to life, to fill his loneliness, and cure his ills.

Only he had been attached to the family house in the San Angel district of Mexico City. Only he, Juan Francisco. He'd cried for his father's return after he left and never came back. As time went by, the others departed, too. First, his sister Gertrude took his love and the most real part of him with her into her hallucinatory world. Their secret love could have saved him. Then later, his mother left. His gods had abandoned him and he remained attached to what no longer existed. They had carried away his roots. After they had all departed, he became aware of his growing repulsion for existence and began to distance himself from life.

In his art, he told Fiedler, he tried to recreate the former togetherness, now evaporated into the polluted atmosphere over the Valley of México, the togetherness hidden in the entangled masses, enigmatic and inscrutable, in the center of his huge dark canvases.

In his loneliness Juan Francisco Alvarez consciously began painting his solitude. He came to believe that his solitude, fearsome and loathsome as it was, was not only his weapon and his defense against the world. His solitude was his art. It was himself. "That's why we Mexicans are the world's best painters," he boasted. "Our solitude!" Since he was cut off from togetherness with what once was and is no more San Miguel was only a temporary haven, an exile.

"I think I'll go talk with old Professor Fiedler this morning," he said at the same moment the idea came to him. It was the one place he could talk all he wanted. "He doesn't have anything to do anyway. I've never seen another patient there."

Fiedler was not as old as Juan Francisco portrayed him. But his obesity and his thin gray hair, turned in lips, horn-rimmed glasses, eternally rumpled suits, and his elephantine movements had made him old at forty. They had always spoken German together, which both spoke fluently: Fiedler from his German parents' home, the German School and studies in Vienna, and Juan Francisco from the German schools he and Gertrude had frequented from kindergarten to university. The German language seemed to have set him and Gertrude apart, isolated them from the rest. From the start his and Gertrude's loneliness—together, sought for, shared—had been the loneliness that counted. The loneliness that conditioned his life … after father left. Together, they had filled their isolation.

"The last time you asked me why I reject the concept of duty," Juan Francisco said. They were sitting on a second floor terrace between two huge palms, surrounded by exotic flowers and plants that made him nervous because of his various undetermined allergies.

"Yes?" the German said.

Juan Francisco watched Fiedler's fattish hand with the stubby German fingers hover around his nose, touching the fat bulb. Fiedler wanted to pick it. Juan Francisco followed the finger with his eyes. Would he stick it up a nostril and begin his search for a glob? Disgusting finger. Disgusting Fiedler. Yet it was the one thing that made him Fiedler. 'Nose-picker,' he called him mentally.

"It was because of the German school. Remember how we all called it the penitentiary. Its severity drove a cleft between us Mexicans and the Germans in the school. Duty and all that malarkey never took on me. I still don't believe that there's some implicit morality in doing one's duty … although I often do it."

"So why do you do it then, your duty?"

"That's what's so maddening, Fiedler. Duty is so oppressive. So non-Mexican. So I began thinking then ... "

"Then? When?"

"When they all left ... when I was alone at home. Just the servants and I were left. I began telling myself I had to have the courage to see myself without that bourgeois veneer of 'I did my duty'. I didn't want to become self-righteous. I should've been, abandoned by everyone like that. I did feel like a martyr. Alone. But I ... you know I detest self-righteousness. I suppose I linked duty and righteousness with God."

"What's that?" Fiedler said. "What's that about duty and God?"

"You always want to come back to Him, Fiedler. I just threw out that word. I don't know Him. He doesn't show me any mercy."

"And you don't care! What about after-death then? He! He! He! You who say you have no problem with death."

Juan Francisco laughed sardonically also. It was the German's weak point. "Well, Professor, I don't care anymore about after-death than I do about pre-birth. What do you think of that? It's all darkness. I only know that I exist now. You know, Fiedler, maybe we're not as Mexican as we think, you and I. Or is that the way Mexicans really think?"

"So where do you think you belong then? Nowhere? Have you no roots? Do you call San Miguel roots?" Fiedler asked sarcastically.

We always come back to that, Juan thought. What are we doing here anyway? Fiedler must have wondered about that. Poor Fiedler! He knows everything about me—everything except the truth about Gertrude and me. No wonder he's always on the wrong track with me. He thinks that because I speak German and went to the same school as him that I'm like him and the others.

"San Miguel?" Juan said. "Don't make me laugh. I mean I walk up the stairs to my mother's apartments on tiptoe. I knock lightly on the door. I'm afraid to disturb. A stranger is now the *Hausherr*. The host.

He commands up there. He's the king. And I'm a visitor. A guest in my own mother's house! I'm a ghost. She has abandoned me again. I'm again an exile, living in the servants' quarters. How can I disturb them? Maybe they're fucking. I don't even know who I am down there. Sometimes during the night I don't even know where I am. So I just hang onto Marisa's tits for my life. And during the day I stagger and stumble around.... Roots seem so old-fashioned anyway."

"Then what is there? You have to be someplace, no?"

"What do I have? I don't have anything. Nothing except my painting. Maybe not even that." How satisfying, he thought, to be able to let down his guard and wallow in the self-pity that had been forbidden ground at home.

He stared fixedly at Fiedler as if daring nose-picker whose index finger was poised just under his left nostril. Caught in the act again, the psychiatrist jerked his hand down.

"*Und? Was denn*?" Fiedler said.

"What does it matter? Nothing! Nothing! I'm just bored. No! You know what I am, Fiedler? I'm disinterested. Not yet indifferent. But today at least, disinterested. Disinterested in what remains of my Mexicanness. Disinterested in the future. Sometimes, Fiedler, I ... I'm ashamed of being Mexican. But if I'm not Mexican then what am I?"

Juan Francisco had begun telling himself during his nighttime vigils that if he could truly become indifferent, if, since he was incapable of the stupid formal courtesy of his people ... if he could learn to remain silent, at least that, he could be truly independent. Independent in his solitude. That's what he strove to paint on top of those huge dark backgrounds—those tiny spectral figures and symbols in which he saw his own immortality.

"Indifferent? Quite frankly, my young friend, your aspiration to indifference seems at odds with your hypochondriac self. Then what about all your ills?"

"Why, you're supposed to cure those, Herr Doktor. Is that not why I'm here?" Juan smirked but pronounced the words sweetly. With that he knew he'd nailed old nose-picker to his cross. It was as good as backhanding Roberto across the chessboard. It was even better.

He was standing indecisively at the curve at the top of Calle San Francisco. Oh, *Cristo Salvador*, I can't face the studio again today. I can't go to the café, either. I don't want to go into that foreign land downtown. Where is one supposed to go? Where can I go?

Unthinking, he turned up the hill toward his secret place. As he passed under the arch and into the trash-filled park he smiled at the signs warning not to dump trash. He followed the path through the narrow valley behind the abandoned castle and the luxury hotel with its terraces and pools. Climbing steadily, he entered the fields of cacti and mesquite trees and wild undergrowth and white dirt, a savage territory between the hills, crisscrossed by white cactus-lined paths made by people from the poor quarters on their way to the plain above. He sat down in a shaded clearing and looked around.

"My place," he said aloud. "Alone, isolated, secure."

He stared at a low terrace of cacti that rose up uncompromisingly before him. They were so different close at hand. What from the road seemed to be a mass of green thickets, from here seemed like life itself—throbbing, thriving, and surviving, both receiving the sun of life and giving life. They were his. He had read that some forms of cactus under certain controlled conditions could survive on the moon. It had to do with oxygen. They didn't need much of it. The magueys. The agave. The noble plant. They provided needles for sewing, fiber for paper, clothing, baskets, medicine, roof thatching, fertilizer, fructose, and above all pulque, mezcal and tequila. You could construct a new human existence with the cactus. The wild plants seemed more real than human life. He could dedicate his life to the cactus. His real life, he thought, was up here on the desolate cactus plain. Alone with his fearful homeless soul that hung onto Marisa's tits for salvation—the crying, searching, falling, emerging, swearing soul, in search of solitude. He, alone and fearful of the wild dogs, on the tableland of cactus surmounted by the white plain of opaque impenetrable dust. The eternal dust of Mexico. The dust that attacks eyes, ears, mouth and the very breath of life. The dust that suffocates. The dust of darkness. The dust of death.

"*Bueno*," he said aloud, squinting toward the evening sun. "It's not only the darkness. It's also *your* mystery, Father Sun. It's the dark and the light." The sun, he knew, could resolve the unthinkable. The sun, the darkness, the cacti, the invisible vipers, they promise me the real world.

A stray dog passed. It stopped, sniffed, stared at him—perhaps perplexed to see a human being here—pissed on a plant, wagged its tail, and moved uphill along the man-made path. Strange things. But for the dog the encounter was already forgotten. It's when you're alone, Juan Francisco thought, helpless and impotent, that the desire to play some outstanding individual role returns. To perform some heroic act, something wild and mad. In order to first deviate and then return to find again your place and be received again into the arms of your fellow human beings. To be different—in order to return to the others. In order to be like the others. He knew he desperately needed the earthliness, the great act of individuality, to reaffirm his human link. First, individuality—then, the rejoining. In that order. Yet how he detested his contrived individuality and flamboyance for flamboyance's sake. His flamboyance was his talk, he knew. He was a show-off, scandalous, quarrelsome, vehement, implausible, nonsensical. His exuberance and his boldness, his rebellion and his diversity—and his solitude—should only go into his painting. To others, he knew, his life style seemed flamboyant. To himself, slovenly. Of course, there were other forms of individuality— real forms like the Hitlers of this world—but being an individual on those extremes was, he admitted, hardly worth the price.

Nevertheless, there were other more personal acts. Like … like he could kill the usurper. Esteban the swine. No? No?

But why? Why was he, at his age, still a stranger to life? Luckily, his abnormality had made him feel blessed that he was not numbered among all those countless, in-tune-with-themselves, normal people. They were the real foreigners. He felt only distancing disdain for them, the normal ones. He was devoid of one iota of envy for their ordered, sane, directed lives, although sometimes he admitted to Fiedler that, yes, it was a consolation to think that we're all ultimately headed in the same direction anyway. How he detested his mortality.

Most people at least start out in normality, attuned to life, before somewhere along the way they let down their guard and let go their sanity and allow their real selves—their mad, uncontrolled and uncontrollable wild selves—to surface.

I instead seem to have started out in abnormality. Never attuned to anything.

Yet what would have happened in my life had they not all abandoned me there in the big house in San Angel? Father promised us paradise—before he reneged and died a lonely death. If Father had made good on his promises, maybe I, Juan Francisco, would never have become a fugitive. Oh, I had to flee from threatening captivity ...only to become the prisoner I am today. He remembered the moments. His contacts with real life were like stepping into another world, into the oddball world that he had dedicated himself to denying, challenging, antagonizing. He'd thought of his move to San Miguel as a move toward sanity—toward a semblance of order and self-discipline. His return to his mother was another attempt to start life anew. From the recesses of his consciousness he recalled how he'd once felt compelled to get a grip on things. To get a handle on life—even though he still didn't know what he would've done with it had he succeeded. The ordered condition he imagined probably didn't exist. But what would it be if it did? A generalized awareness? A consciousness of everything? That could be more terrible than his out-of-tuneness, his waywardness, his solitude. In his case, it would mean an awareness of good and evil at the same time! Then how would he choose? How could he deal with life if he had a grip on everything? Old Fiedler had once said that would be like holding the spark of mankind in your own hands.

His father's death in a distant land had upset such aspirations. For he had been his son's hold on life. The promise of his redemption. How he'd loved him. Worshipped him. He still did. As far as emotions and feelings go, that was already a lot. His father's death didn't fit into this explanation of life. It wasn't fair.

He had always lied to Fiedler. You have just come to understand life and suddenly you are face to face with the enigma of death. That's the way things really go. The idea that his father was no more, that he had no future, was unbearable. Intolerable. Juan Francisco's grip on life went up in smoke the day his father lost his future. When Gertrude, his heart, deserted him, he became a spectator to the slow, gradual, then accelerating decline and near disappearance of his own capacity for affection or for charity—or even for tolerance.

And now he had to hold onto Marisa's tits for dear life.

Walking jerkily downhill in his uncoordinated gait, Juan Francisco raised his eyes at the screech of metal scraping metal and the roar of revving motors echoing up toward him between the high stonewalls. A crowd, yelling, shouting and gesticulating wildly, was gathered at the narrow passage of the cobblestone street between the high steps of the school on one side and apartment houses on the other. Traffic was stopped. The street was blocked. A downhill bus on one side was jammed against a gas truck headed up the hill.

Women standing around a small boy were trying to remove his torn and bloody blue and white school uniform. His chest and face were bleeding. He was crying hysterically and flailing his arms. He'd been trapped against the wall by the bus.

"*No quiero, no quiero*," the boy kept screaming. "*Me muero, me muero*." I'm dying. I'm dying.

"*No, no, muchacho*," the women were saying, "*no te mueres, estás bien, estás bien.*"

Two men were pinned against the wall, crushed in a vise of steel and cement from their chests to their knees. The face of one was fiery red, his eyes jumping from their sockets. The other's face was deathly white, his eyes closed. The faces of life and death. They had tipped the bus to free the boy but then were themselves trapped. The bus was stuck fast. The gas truck couldn't move. No one knew what to do.

Sirens announced the arrival of firemen and police. Juan Francisco began shouting: "Do something, do something." But the authorities pushed him aside while the chiefs consulted. The crowd fell silent.

"Move the bus, move the bus," he shouted anyway. "That man is dying. He's dead." Only once had he seen death so near—a man lying dead on a fast highway, motionless on the pavement. It was the solitude of death that struck him. He stared as the same solitude settled on the pale face of the man with his eyes closed. He was about to witness the passage from life to nothingness. The spark of life was departing. It emerged through the man's mouth and passed through his breath in a gurgle. He felt the choking sensation, then saw its UFO-like, smoky blue flight to some other place.

From ladders propped against the wall, dark wiry men descended to the bus level. Their feet against the wall for leverage, they gradually tilted the bus another few inches while their companions below extracted the heroes-victims from the mortal trap.

Juan Francisco smiled. Mexican ingenuity had triumphed.

The man with the red face gasped, coughed, cried, staggered a few steps, turned to the crowd and laughed loud. People clapped. He was alive.

Juan Francisco observed the dead one with the pale face lying on a stretcher. They had covered him with a blanket up to his chin. Suddenly his eyes twitched. Miraculously, out of blackness, out of nothingness, with his eyes still closed, the man smiled. Life returned to him. Juan Francisco watched the spirit, no longer free, returning through his open receptive mouth. He had recaptured life. The man was no longer alone.

The early night air still conserved a residue of the sun's warmth when a shaken Juan Francisco stepped onto the sprawling roof terrace. Cooking smells hung in the evening air. Tables were set on the terrace and in the salon. People in sweaters or shawls over their shoulders were chattering here and there. It was the night of the barbecue.

"Hola, Johnny," said his mother and kissed him on both cheeks. "I was worried about you."

In a far corner next to the rear wall, Esteban was cooking spare ribs and sausages and corn on the cob. He was wearing an irritating white chef's cap. He smiled and waved his big cook's fork. Juan Francisco didn't respond.

"Where's Marisa?" he asked sullenly, looking around among Elizabeta's friends. He had no idea who they were.

"I don't believe Marisa will be coming," his mother said hesitantly in English, the common language of her parents, which she had always spoken with her children. "She had an urgent call from home. Uh ... Johnny, she left this for you," Elizabeta said, taking a small envelope from her jacket pocket. "Now don't let it upset you!"

He stepped closer to the light and read the few words: "*Querido Juan Francisco, mi madre está mala y tengo que ir a casa con urgenza. Te voy a llamar cuando pueda regresar. Besitos, Marisa.*"

"Kisses! She sends me kisses, the little puta!" he shouted rushing toward his mother and waving the note. People around the terrace fell silent. "She claims her mother is sick. That whore! I'll bet she returned to that Nacho or whatever his name was. Leaving me alone. Not even the courage to tell me to my face. Typical of her kind. Ah, just wait till I get my hands on her again. But she won't dare come back to San Miguel ... she'll pay ..."

"Shush, Johnny, please. The others! Don't play your usual demented self. Have some regard for me. She'll come back."

"No, she'll never come back. She's dead too. Traitoress. Liar. Just like Gertrude. They never come back, never come back, they all go, they all go. Poppy left. Gertrude left. Now you're going, too. Again! When are you leaving? When? Don't you have the courage to tell me? I should've known. That one day you would leave, again. They all leave. And your Johnny stays alone."

Suddenly, in the stillness crashing around him, he felt ridiculous. He made a brusque movement in the direction of Esteban. Elizabeta put her hand on his arm. He should kill Esteban. He would like to push him off the roof, or crush his face into his own fire. He shook off his mother's hand. He screamed inside. He saw his own violence reflected in her eyes. She was afraid. His insanity, he knew, lay shallow. It was visible. That thing in him frightened the others. In his solitude, he'd clung to her, as he'd clung to Gertrude, as he clung to Marisa's tits, and to the life raft of the exhibition. The exhibition, out there in the real world where things worked. Where people married, had children, rose early for work, lived and died.

But Father had betrayed him. As Gertrude had betrayed and abandoned him. Now Marisa, wandering from man to man and offering her tits in succor, was betraying him. His chess companion had betrayed him with a never made move. Now his mother was betraying him with that *cabrón* Esteban. And Fiedler, trustworthy old Fiedler, was content to sit there on his terrace with his finger up his nose.

The miracle at the wreck had raised his hopes. Only a few minutes ago, in this Sodom-Gomorrah, he had seen Jesus dead and resurrected. But it was deception and hallucination.

He glared around him, his eyes unseeing. These are mysterious events. They must presage extraordinary happenings. My old world is surely ending. I perceive a premonition of new miracles in the air. The portents are here. Only I, Juan Francisco Alvarez, perceive them. I wait for them. Only I continue the struggle. Now, in the big house on the hill, I, the solitary soldier, will resist. Isolation is my salvation. It's the admission price. My loneliness is my father's gift. A sacred gift. Oh, my generous father, he paid for it with his own life. He didn't destroy me. He gave me life. How could I succeed in my isolation with Marisa? She needs only to love and be loved. But I don't have that capacity. She was right to escape. I must stay. For a moment, in despair, he accepted it—Father, Mother, Gertrude and Marisa would never return. Time had stopped. He had no past. No future. Only the solitary present remained.

He turned back to Esteban and frowned. Slowly, he approached him with his fists clenched. His mother grabbed his arm, but he pushed her off so violently that she fell, luckily, onto a couch.

Esteban dropped his cooking utensils and backed away, terror in his eyes. When Juan Francisco was a foot away from him he grinned wolfishly and whispered, "*cabrón!*"

Then he turned away, grasped his sobbing mother's hands to help her up, and kissed her passionately on the lips. Then he left, still grinning his mad grin.

CHESS AND LIANA

1.

Lead weighed heavy on his eyeballs. Countless espressos worn off, their absence dragging him from the peak of his matinal inspiration downwards toward oblivion. Toward non-existence. Noonday light filtered through the jungle turned blue. He tried to be rational while the jungle surrounding him beat against his ears. It beat and throbbed. Beat and throbbed. In the shrinking circles of his mind he searched for a hold against the liana. Liana was encircling and enveloping and blanketing and cloaking the van, occupying his world. Liana popped around his head and into his deadened mind. Liana omnipresent. Carnivorous liana engulfing and devouring him, too. Breath abandoned his lungs, his eyes lost their vision, rivulets of his sweat ran down his neck, time faded and seemed to end.

I had always thought Pier Paolo's corporal space too confining for his spirit. His body was too small to contain him. He needed more living space. From the portico I watched his dusty ramshackle van battle its way through the wild vegetation encroaching on the gully-ridden dirt roadway leading to the door of his country house. The Ho Chi Minh Trail, we called it. Branches of spontaneous trees and unidentifiable bushes and thickets and vines slapped against the windshield, then gradually slid away. Framed between his two hands clutching the steering wheel, his reddened swollen face emerged from the August heat and his internal agitation. At the same moment he broke free of the jungle assault his bulging burning eyes briefly met mine, concealing as best he could his derision and irony toward life.

Pier Paolo climbed down from the van slowly, slightly bent, his belly drooping over the tight belt holding up his jeans covering skinny bowed legs. Unsmiling he waved a hand at me. He lit a cigarette and as on each arrival home he stopped to stare down the valley toward Florence as if measuring the distance he'd just covered. He turned back to me, wiped his forehead, pulled at his scraggly beard, slapped at his neck spuriously, inhaled deeply and still straight-faced, said disinterestedly:

"*Qual é la situazione zanzare oggi?*" What's the mosquito situation today?

"They're all resting after their last attack early this morning," I said, fixing on the red veins crossing the bulbs of his eyeballs. Suspended precariously over red rims his eyes were in fiery contrast with the perennial black circles under them. I thought his blood pressure must have been hovering at around 200.

"*Paranoico*!" he grunted.

Mosquitoes never touched Pier Paolo. He asked in jest since I live in fear of mosquitoes, only one of which was too many for me. As far as he was concerned there were 'only a few' in all of Fiesole. For him, the mosquitoes infesting the bushes and woods around the country house, incubating in the pools of stagnant water remaining from forgotten rains and waiting in ambush in the dry fields of olive orchards, were nonexistent. No, mosquitoes never touched him. Or if they did he ignored them as he did most of nature. Though he claimed to love dogs and cats and occasionally stopped to pet one or the other, he seemed in general impervious to the flora and the fauna.

As far as he was concerned, the spontaneous jungle from which he had just emerged did not exist.

While Pier Paolo put on the water for pasta, I poured the Chianti and began setting up the chessboard under the portico. On the days he returned to his house on the hill for lunch we would start a game while the water boiled. Afterwards, he would need very few of his lightning moves to checkmate me. He had held the Fiesole championship for the last three years. Losing, I hoped to absorb some of his mastery.

After two years in a commune and three years working with spastic children, this summer Pier Paolo had returned to carpentry. He shared a workshop with a friend down in Florence in the workers' district of San Frediano where they made on order country style, manually operated spinning wheels. Nights, he was working on a complex invention of a keyboard with which spastics could type on their computers with their feet.

"Shall I slice the tomatoes?" I asked, knowing his answer in advance.

"I'll do it." He didn't trust my cut. Not that Pier Paolo was a great cook but his summer speciality of fresh tomatoes, sliced just so, spread over the spaghetti, was my favorite dish. We ate it every second day that summer while our wives spent their days at a swimming pool complex in the hills in the direction of Bologna.

His grunts and curt answers were deceptive. He didn't make the drive up the Fiesole hill just because I was a summer guest. He felt no obligation toward me his brother-in-law. Some days he didn't come at all. I knew where he was those days. But Pier Paolo welcomed the chance to eat pasta and drink wine and play chess under the portico without the presence of his wife who always seemed a reminder of his failure as a husband and provider, of his shortcomings in day-to-day life.

Though they adored him, his parents and his wife expected more of him. His friends expected more of him. Everyone expected more expressions of his genius. And more rewards, too.

No matter how one looked at his situation, Pier Paolo just didn't live up to expectations. By normal standards he would be considered a failure in life. A law school drop-out. A list of abandoned jobs and firings behind him. A life of quick enthusiasms and sudden apathy. A reluctant husband—he'd only married to satisfy his parents. No children, and according to my sister-in-law, Lalla, he had little interest in sex.

Lacking any sense at all of possession of anything or anyone, Pier Paolo was at the same time a total egoist; he was both totally generous and totally egocentric. His head was in the clouds, everybody said. A dreamer. His inventions of things already invented were legion. He'd devoted weeks to making by hand a special wooden airplane, an upside down plane, wings in the back and tail fins in the front, a blue yellow red purple airplane never seen before—it was hanging from the kitchen ceiling. Meanwhile he was an unstoppable talker, polemical on every possible subject, banal or otherwise—Was the pasta al dente or overdone? Was Bologna or Arezzo closer to Florence? Did the city of Florence really care about its disabled youth? Was Italy's government a democracy or a dictatorship?—in any discussion he was capable of unbridled fits of anger that then sputtered and ended as suddenly as they had exploded.

Pier Paolo was, how can I say it? he was both loveable and unbearable. Sometimes you just had to get up and leave and try to put him behind you. Not as easy as it sounds for he was somehow always present, either his expansive physical self or his invasive spirit. If he was not always physically present in the country house on the hill of Fiesole, he was certainly the chief topic of conversation.

"This is the life," I said, as we ate his pasta al pomodoro.

These were good days. My favorite vacation. No traffic-packed highways for us. No packed beaches and Apennine mountain paths as crowded as Central Park on Sunday morning.

Pier Paolo was silent.

The cloudless sky rose, borderless, limitless, endless. The hills around spread like a spider's web, rolling down to Firenze below, another chain climbing toward the north, speckled by white and pastel villas with red tile roofs and olive and fruit orchards on their flanks and pines and cypresses on their crests. The sudden barking of dogs and the multiple responses echoing through the hills, the sound of a flute from across the highroad, the rasping of a motorcycle, the audible sagging of vines under the weight of ripened grapes hanging from the roof, the chatter of rabbits from behind the barn, and again dead silence before a single shot shattered the hillside peace.

"The women at the crowded pool and we on top of the world's most beautiful hill," I insisted. "The people who've always lived up here know a thing or two. Some people just seem to know how to live."

"Fortunate the man who doesn't have to learn to live," Pier Paolo muttered, lighting a cigarette even before finishing the pasta. "Spoiled as I once was, my parents thought everything was arranged for me."

"You're lucky. That left you more time for real things."

"No, no!" he said, his wild eyes bulging from their sockets, his face on fire. He puffed at his cigarette and inhaled deeply. "I even had to learn to despair … like an autistic child."

"You learned well," I said facetiously. "Look at you now!"

"They wanted me to be at ease. Carefree. It was their serenity that was so frustrating, their sincerity toward life. Early on I *was* at ease … but dissatisfied. I was just my father's son. Until one day … well, until everything changed. And I came to want desperation."

"Still, it seems you always do the right things." I pushed aside the plates and positioned the chessboard between us. It was my turn to play with white.

"You're dead wrong. My life is a calvary. My only hope is to die young," he said, the familiar faraway look in his suddenly calmed eyes. "I'll die from my obsessions."

"Absurd," I said and opened as always with the king's pawn. I looked up at him and in that moment I seemed to see straight into his life as never before.

"That might be," he said, and moved his king's knight to threaten my pawn, which constituted the substance of the rest of the game—his black pieces threatening my white wherever they might be. That was his winning system. "They asked me again to join them. Fulvio … and the others. They want to resurrect what died years ago."

"You mean his gang of would-be terrorists?"

I moved my pawn forward, foolishly trying to menace *him*. Without a thought he flipped his knight to the side where it would sit like a hawk ready to swoop down on any enemy pawns venturing into his territory.

"I said no just as I did fifteen years ago. I still wonder if I did wrong. The Arno River is still polluted. We're producing garbage faster than they can find secret places in the south to dump it. The Fascists run things. The city has no money for social problems. And now, what with the whole town occupied year round by tourists—they're even up here in Fiesole—a little bit of home-made terrorism might chase them away."

"*Beccati questo*!" Take this, I said and moved my king's bishop to threaten his knight. Without blanching he brought out his queen's knight and looked at me expectantly. I didn't know what to do then … his power was already advancing … he had two devious knights ready to pounce … I had nothing.

Pier Paolo once told me he loved chess because it was so different from life. In chess one false move ruins you. In life the hardest part is knowing exactly where you went wrong. Can you ever look back and pinpoint the moment you erred? Can you see clearly where you took the wrong turn? It's difficult enough to discern starting points but impossible to establish turning points. Yet he still wondered if there was not always one great error, one misdeed, where we go wrong? An error that then conditions our lives? That then never releases us? And in retrospect are we not aware that it might have been otherwise? He said it was not mere rhetoric but a matter of conscience. The conscience of human beings that separates us from animal beings. And that makes us need to be extraordinary. His aim was to leave his mark. And the thought of failure in that too was his terror and his torment.

Meanwhile, the surreptitious move of a pawn here, the unexpected dash of a rook the length of the board, and he suddenly had all his power up front—both knights, his bishops posed strategically as diagonal threats, and his queen waiting patiently to strike. I viewed my muddled army—troops disorganized, chaotic, here one pawn behind the other, there a bishop blocked behind my own knight. Casually Pier Paolo began picking off my pawns, the other knight, an unawares rook. In the end he checkmated me simultaneously with both his queen and a bishop.

"Bobby Fisher," he muttered … and named his Russian opponent.

2.

Where was it? he wondered. The right word. No, not the word. The right action. The right thing. The right color. Shards of colored lights were glittering and glimmering and shimmering. The green of human vision. The celeste of the sky. The white of innocence. Like her eyes glittering in the lamplight. She wanted more of life. Why not more? Why couldn't he give more? She didn't understand the liana when he told her. She could never understand the threat. Or his fear. Liana on Fiesole, everyone asked? Liana on Fiesole. Man-eating liana in his mind. The Fiesole sounds he heard, too. The sound of the gate. Clack, clack, clack. The gate he'd built for the dogs. In and out, in and out of the barn. The hinges rusted. It was the dogs. It was the breeze. Light breezes from the hills of the Via Bolognese. Cypresses waving. Breezes calling across the hills. Olive orchards, villas, the old highway … and the woman. She was calling, calling, calling. From the hills of the Via Bolognese, she was calling.

Fulvio had said, 'Join us!' He said, no! To political activists today, he said, no! To the movements, he said, no! Now he only talked a life. But he had his dreams. Night and day he dreamed. He passed easily from dream to dream. Dreams of words and action and power and violence and colors and lights … and her eyes.

Pier Paolo was staring across the hills. I knew where he was looking. I knew what it meant. Her name was Isabel. Peruvian, an artist who painted graceful children. Isabel lived on the Via Bolognese. He had told me that she was usually half nude. Topless, he said. She showed off her breasts. Her brown brown breasts. Pier Paolo said it was her insecurity and her maternal instinct. She liked to hear that. He said her topless life style was her art; she painted graceful children, full of grace and innocence.

Fulvio had told me Isabel was very active sexually, with or without him—she drove him to the limits. And to desperation. We all thought that was the reason Pier Paolo was crazed. At first he had treated her like a daughter—she came to their house in Fiesole, he and Lalla talked about her freely, she was one of the family.

That was until one day when they were all lunching under the portico she insisted on taking off her shirt. Then it became incest. He was obsessed. His incestuous obsession, Pier Paolo called it.

I stared at Pier Paolo staring toward the Via Bolognese. He was again ablaze. His face reminded me of the time some years back at Saturnia. We were all burned that day at the hot mineral springs—the August sun and the sulphur waters. Pier Paolo who avoids the sun like the plague was on fire, his eyes white, his lips purple. After drinks in the village café, he started across the street, stopped in the middle and held his hand to his heart, a stricken look of terror on his flaming face. I rushed to him with a chair from the café. I can still see him sitting there in the middle of the street, an occasional car passing us in both directions—burned by sun and sulphur, immobile, terrorized, his hand posed on his pounding breast, he is looking up at me as if to ask if his time is already up. It was surprising because of his usual scorn for death—he didn't care, he said, his two plus packs of filterless cigarettes each day, his high blood pressure, his defiance of doctors.

"You thinking of going to Bologna?" I said, trying to disguise any unintentional irony in my voice. "You keep looking that way."

"*Se tu solo sapessi*! If you only knew! But I can't. I can't. Just look at me!" His ballooned eyes white, he took a long drink of wine, threw away his cigarette and lit another. 'And to do what?'

None of this story was secret. Everybody in the household on Fiesole knew about his fixation on Isabel. Pier Paolo's parents knew. His mother-in-law, that is, Lalla's and my wife's mother, or, *la nonna* as we all called her, knew. We all knew about Pier Paolo and Isabel. We knew the ups and downs. We knew about his hang-ups. And he knew we knew. There were no more secrets about Isabel than about the man Pier Paolo called Lalla's lover-fiancé. There was no embarrassment when Pier Paolo answered the phone and called Lalla—"It's your fiancé!" he would say, not only without irony but with no attempt to mask the joy he felt that she had someone.

Telephones were important in the house on the hill of Fiesole. The howling dogs and screeching cats and rumbling motorcycles on the highroad, and the rustling of the expanding and swelling and lengthening liana on the Ho Chi Minh trail. And the telephone calls from and to their respective fiancés.

La nonna, who detested Pier Paolo for what he was and for taking away her Lalla, said he was a *frocio*, that is, a queer. She was convinced that Fulvio was *his* lover. So if she answered the phone and it was Fulvio, she would call out to Pier Paolo: "It's your fiancé."

3.

Liana is a parasite incapable of supporting its own weight. It roots in the ground and creeps around tree trunks and branches. With little seed reserves of its own, liana develops great stalk extensions. Thread-like and weak, to survive it has to cling to other plants with its almost extraneous roots or its organs of connection or its long branches. Liana has an exceptional capacity for lengthening. Its stalks and stems and tentacles take on odd forms and shapes, like tapes or spirals, corresponding to the anomalies in its whole anatomic structure—its twisting and its torsions within its impenetrable mass. Its habitat is the rain forest. So what is it doing here, Pier Paolo wondered? He remembered that unlike other plants liana is half uprooted. It does not want to stay in one place. It wants more. Nature, he thought, is the antithesis of man. The divine is in man, not in nature which is neither good nor evil—or is it? The divine in man is in a battle with nature, against its meaninglessness. Man—ever searching for meaning. Is man's mission to destroy unfeeling nature?

Early the next morning from under my window I heard the chainsaw and the sounds of thrashing and hacking and cutting mixed with grunts and oaths. A rush of the saw and his muttered '*porca Madonna*' that *la Nonna* detested and for which she condemned Pier Paolo to hellfire. I knew it was him.

Marisa next to me was in the dead of her night. The household was quiet. I crept to the window and looked down at him. Bare to the waist, Pier Paolo was surrounded by piles of hacked and torn and uprooted vines and creepers and stalks and tree branches; yet he seemed to have advanced no more than about a meter in his attack on the Ho Chi Minh trail. His arm holding the saw was pointed toward a spontaneous tree engulfed by liana hanging over the roadway. He looked up at me, his face flushed and a crazed smile on his purple lips.

"*Porca Madonna*!" he said. "Nature is winning. It has eyes … it's watching me. Its mouth is watering."

"I'll come down and help," I said softly.

"No need," he said. "*Mi arrendo*. I surrender."

He turned the saw on anyway and waved it half-heartedly toward the tree victim before dropping his arm and walking away from the battle scene, the saw still whirring away.

Shortly afterwards I heard him on the downstairs phone.

"Who is it?" Lalla called from the next room.

"His fiancé," *la nonna* said from down the hall.

"I'm not coming to work," Pier Paolo was saying. "I'm too sick."

Lalla groaned, "Not again!"

Everyone knew what that meant. Pier Paolo was again taking to bed as he did every three or four months. Sometimes for days and weeks he lived in pyjamas. Lying in his upstairs room or on the couch in the living room watching TV around the clock. He would watch everything with equal interest, as if he were a just arrived New Guinean aborigine. He watched quiz shows, talk shows, reality shows, cooking and gardening shows, travelogues about Zanzibar or the Caribbean, soap operas, and all the advertising spots and TV sales, the vilest, the very worst, the dark pit of television. And all the while smoking and waiting to be served his meals. Then, all of a sudden, it would end—he would get up, take a shower, dress, and drive down to Florence to see his mother.

"What's up?" I asked when that afternoon I found him stretched out on the couch, a cigarette in his hand and an overflowing ashtray and the wireless phone on his stomach. He was following a women's talk show about lovers, jealousy and separation.

"*Il male non esiste.* Evil does not exist," he said, just like that, matter-of-factly, without taking his eyes off the screen.

"Why do you say that?"

"Those dogs howling out there aren't evil. Nor are people evil, deep-down. They're just misled … or they forget they're good."

"Do you want to play chess?" I said, trying to change the subject.

"I'm dissatisfied but I'm not unhappy. So I try to create a little evil around me so someone will get mad … and then I can be unhappy."

He looked up at me standing over him and asked, "Does sex disturb you?"

When I said sometimes, he said that it gnawed away at him, that it was always there.

That same evening just before dinner we were pleasantly surprised when he rose from the couch, took his usual post-illness shower, dressed and left—we all knew, headed for the Via Bolognese.

"Thank God!" Lalla said.

"Off to his fiancé," *la Nonna* said.

4.

Where to go? Images, visions, shadows and reflections flashed for an instant across his eyes and in one bolt vanished, he knew irretrievable and absolute. Briefly they existed … as reality. Oh, to be able to decelerate the tempo, the march of time, to reach out and pluck the images and reflections like fruit. To have a season. Oh, the torment of images! A day of his time. A winter's day of time. A muffled horn from the highroad in the early morning. A light flickering in the fog. The rush through the moaning liana. The blue neon at the bar in San Domenico where he breakfasted. The old woman selling chestnuts on Piazza della Signoria. The apartment houses along the Arno south of Ponte Vecchio. His own reflection in the rain-splattered window of the shop in San Frediano. And then: the stillness of the room when she sleeps. In the evening snow falling on Fiesole. The valley before the Via Bolognese. A day of time. The images were his. Beauty, romance and mystery. Sadness, pain and fear.

It was the fear. The fear in his guts. Trembling fears. Pier Paolo held up a hand to the windshield to observe his trembling. It ran up his arm to his shoulders and down his spine. It was alive. Fear was an animal. So uncontrollably animal-like, anti-human. He knew he was right not to trust nature.

But instinct? Can I not trust instinct as always? As in chess where instinct seldom betrayed him. He twisted his hand and clenched and unclenched a fist and recalled the tournament years before when he first won the championship. It was the decisive move—to sacrifice his knight or his bishop? The dilemma. Reason told him to give up the knight in case his plan backfired. His instinct said sacrifice the bishop and strike home for the checkmate. His instinct was right.

Now Pier Paolo observed his trembling hand and knew instinct had deserted him.

Isabel was waiting on the rear terrace facing Fiesole. The scene was so familiar. Isabel—tanned, long-legged, a purple flower in her long hair, barefoot, topless. On her easel, a nude girl child with a purple flower in her hair, a chain of small white flowers around her neck, long tanned legs.

She put down her brush, wiped her hands, stood up and took him by the hand.

"Come," she said.

Stretched out beside Isabel on the wide multi-colored couch in the living room looking out onto the terrace looking out to the valley toward Fiesole, Pier Paolo felt the chaos pressing at his throat like the tentacles of liana. It was the hills of oppressive nature. A confrontation. Fiesole on one hill looking toward the Via Bolognese. The Via Bolognese on another hill looking at Fiesole. Was that all? Was it all the same? With one hand he stroked her breasts but he felt only the bright Peruvian colors under them. And around them. The colors assailed his senses. When Isabel pushed at his pants he thought of the carnivorous liana. Sweat rolled down from under his armpits. He felt himself shrinking.

"Isabel!" Pier Paolo said.

"Again!" Isabel said.

He stood up and pulled her to her feet.

She started to put on a shirt. He stopped her.

Though it was dark he drove without lights. Down the hill from the Via Bolognese, up and down several lower hills, before initiating the final climb up to San Domenico and Fiesole. The heat pressed around them. Fireflies flittered in the bush when they turned off the highroad onto the Ho Chi Minh Trail. Bats rose from scattered roofs here and there. Both van windows were open when they entered the bush.

The night was hot and humid, the hottest in decades, perhaps in centuries. TV weathermen spoke of an exceptional heat wave from North Africa. I turned on the fans, closed hermetically doors and windows, sprayed and put on various anti-mosquito apparatuses. All evening meteorologists continued explaining the dramatic changes in world climate. Hotter summers, colder winters. Sweltering days and nights in Scandinavia and Scotland and Ireland. The glaciers were melting, sea levels rising. Palms and other tropical plants were reported in Milan in the north, and in the Tessin in southern Switzerland, and were beginning their ascent upwards toward the Inn valley. One felt the jungle pressing.

La Nonna shrugged and said she was cold anyway. Lalla and my wife were gradually stripping while I huddled near the electric anti-mosquito appliance pumping its noxious fumes into the living room. The noise of the electric fans, the TV and the usual chatter blotted out everything else and isolated us from the dangerous world outside.

In a bizarre atmosphere of threat and foreboding the whole household retired. Pier Paolo had not returned. No one really expected him. When I looked out our bedroom window, an out-of-season misty rain was falling. Humidity must have been one hundred per cent.

The early morning sky was a heavy leaden gray. When I opened the window the air felt like Panama City in the afternoon. Automatically I looked toward the Ho Chi Minh Trail as if expecting Pier Paolo to arrive at any moment. For a moment I thought I saw a movement in the bush. Or a light trying to penetrate through the green. Or it was a reflection. Like a neon sign blinking on and off, faintly, faintly, but a beacon, a call. I don't know why but I read a Morse SOS.

I crept down the stairs and outside. Silence reigned. Not even the dogs were barking. No movement on the highroad. I felt the strange living presence of the jungle. It seemed to have advanced since yesterday. The branches and tentacles Pier Paolo had cut had vanished.

I stopped at the wall of the green mass. What I had seen as a reflection had become a mere shadow. I seemed to hear a rattle, and a rush inside the bush, on the trail, among the liana. Hesitantly I parted the first tentacles that during the night had enveloped the road in its clutch. Little by little I advanced against raw nature.

The reflection or the light that had become a shadow soon transformed into a solid object. The earth was mushy beneath my feet. Mosquitoes swarmed over me. A bulk began materializing before me. Stems and branches and tentacles of crazily convoluted liana wound round and round it. At knee level a light shone faintly. I was now standing in water. I knew. I leaned forward and saw bits of windows. I knew what it was. I knew what I would find inside. I ripped and pulled at the liana. It resisted. I became frantic and yanked and jerked at the tenacious vines. When the side of the van was cleared, I pressed my face into the gaping hole of the window and peered into the darkened interior.

Liana tentacles had invaded the interior. The two figures were convoluted together with nature. One was atop the other, wrapped into one package. Pier Paolo had always said that liana is deceptive. A carnivorous species tends to first cling to its object as if in adoration, and then devours it.

As my eyes adjusted to the near darkness, I could barely make out only the exposed form of a female breast.

THE FALL

At first it seemed that Ferdinando's problems began when he tore the meniscuses in both knees when he jumped—he subsequently claimed he jumped—from a one-meter high stone wall in his backyard to save his beloved kitten from a savage little dog that, I knew, was really more afraid of the kitten than was the tiny feline of the dog. But my neighbor was a protective type. He said the dog would have torn to pieces his cuddly kitten that was so small—he explained—because as the last of a litter of eight she'd barely made it into life.

The truth of how he injured his knees however differs from his frequently repeated version of the scene that transpired before my very eyes. Since at the time he "jumped" off the wall I was standing nearby—separated only by a wire fence—I observed the entire sequence of events and swear that, first of all, he didn't jump at all. He fell. And hard.

It happened like this: as usual, Ferdinando was a little high from his first bottle of wine of the day. Moreover, he was overweight from too many days, too many weeks and months—and now years—of too many bottles of wine, so that at forty-five, his belly hung far over his belt.

At the time of his fall we were engaged in deep conversation as we always were in those times, I, standing at the fence, and he, perched on the wall. And, to tell the full story, Ferdinando, as was his nature, was also distracted by his own words: he had just pronounced one of his pithy aphorisms which I later noted for future reference—"Though we hardly notice it, a shadow of ourselves always stands just behind us like notes of a piece of music remain hanging in the air for even hours after the music has finished ..."

To my question filtered through the wire fence about the role of his shadow, he said it was the "driving force in his life". So it was in the precise moment that he waved an arm to emphasize his point that he lost his balance, stumbled awkwardly and began his fall off the wall, flailing his long thin arms and kicking his long thin legs, before landing on his feet with the thud of a stomping elephant near the startled but still barking little dog and the screeching kitten.

After his fall, leaning forward toward me with the kitten safely in his arms and kicking at the little dog, he looked at me behind the wire fence and, as if his fall had not even occurred, added to his aphorism. "… like the breath of life remains and hovers over the lifeless but still emptying body for some minutes after death."

That was Ferdinando. Genius or buffoon was unclear. After his fall he walked in a normal gait toward me at the wire fence we both detested and said, "Lucky I didn't land on my head," and handed me the kitten over the fence. "Hold Dolcezza for me while I get rid of this vicious canine. He's a good little dog but goes absolutely bonkers when he so much as sees a feline, especially a little one like Dolcezza."

For most people Ferdinando was not the ideal neighbor. Though a little wacky and often thoughtful of others at the wrong times, he had little respect for common property … especially not for his own. But I had come to love him like a brother.

His beautiful wife, Antonia, had a lot of patience with his eccentricities which he cultivated in his two children both under twelve years old. They pounded up and down the stairs of our adjoining duplex houses at any time of day or night. Then he might suddenly crack down on excessive noise, again aware that I was probably writing on the other side of the dividing walls. And he would yell at the top of his voice to Chiara and Dario to cut out that racket and that otherwise, Giacomo, that is me, *si incazzarebbe*, that I would get fucking mad. On which they would all giggle. And Chiara and Dario would repeat *non far incazzare* Giacomo, *non far incazzare* Giacomo. In any other words don't fuck with me when I'm writing.

When Giulia and I went there for dinner, Antonia served take-out food from the local snack bar on paper plates, while afternoons Chiara and Dario sometimes marched into our house, straight to the refrigerator and helped themselves to any goodies they found.

Ferdinando was one of those persons who know a sketchy lot about many subjects. Since I had lived for a few years in Amsterdam, he liked to tell me stories of the city as the home of Liberalism, "the anti-

Hobbesian city", he called it, that tried to solve the economic problems that made "*the life of man solitary, poor, nasty, brutish and short*", as described in Hobbes' classic *Leviathan*; a world in which nobody could count on anything, and replaced it, for a time, with a society where nothing was virtual; everything was real; and every financial document was backed up by real goods in real warehouses.

I confirmed that I'd read that all of Amsterdam in its Golden Age was one great warehouse. No wonder the world's first stock market was created there; it was due to the successes of the Dutch East India Company in which Dutch people bought shares in real existing things: ships and crews, rubber and spices and coffee and tea arriving in the great port of Amsterdam.

Ferdinando claimed that at Milan's Bocconi University he once wrote a paper on the great pupil of the Liberalism of the philosopher Baruch Spinoza, Johan de Witt, who was the *Stadholder*, the governor of Amsterdam as well as of the whole province of Holland. Ferdinando explained that the godless influence on De Witt of the philosopher of modernity, the Amsterdam-born Portuguese Jew, Bento d'D'Espinoza—trimmed to Spinoza, and Bento changed to the Hebrew, Baruch— was deadly. In the fatal year of 1672, Ferdinando specified, Holland's competitors, England and France, allied in a war to overthrow him and the then richest city in the world.

A half century after they burned Giordano Bruno in Rome for propagating the same philosophies as Spinoza—a God who doesn't think or have pity or watch or feel compassion or answer prayers, a borderless God beyond religions—Dutch stockholders, furious when they saw their fortunes evaporating, their lowlands invaded and crushed by the armies of their perfidious English competitors, rose up against de Witt, stabbed him to death, hanged and quartered him, then burned him and according to legend ate his well-cooked flesh.

Justifiably upset by this fiery end to his ideal of the democratic state, Spinoza re-qualified his original ideal, writing before his own death that: "*Men are of necessity liable to passions and prone to vengeance more than mercy*." The philosopher of liberalism was soon as dead as was liberalism itself after the assault by the armies of the

Monarchy and the Church. Yet over two centuries later, Albert Einstein, on being asked if he believed in God, answered, "*I believe in Spinoza's God ... not in a God who concerns himself with the fates and actions of human beings.*"

Now Ferdinando knew that he was at a turning point in his career just as De Witt had been before his fall. Therefore, and also because of his need to confide in someone, Ferdinando told me that he made more money than he had ever dreamed of as a junior executive in the investment division of the National Insurance House, the NIH, which he noted is quoted on the London stock exchange.

Still, he added with a speciously guilty snicker, he didn't actually even understand actuarial tables. And besides, he confessed, he found little joy in his work.

Once, before his fall from the wall, at a dinner party at his house for two top NIH executives and their wives to which he invited also Giulia and me they served martini cocktails, used their elegant antique fratina table with a linen table cloth and laid tableware that had been in his family for generations.

Later, over coffee and cognac in the more intimate second salon, one of the distinguished executives—by then sloshed by the two or more extra-large Hemingwayan martini cocktails, that is Montgomerys, the strong white Sardinian wine with the shrimp cocktail, bountiful quantities of Montalcino red wines with the meat dishes, some liqueur or the other with deserts, and now his second or third Remy Martin—looking fondly at Ferdinando across the small room, told me in a loud whisper that top company officers were perplexed by my friend, Ferdinando: they still didn't know whether he was an investment genius or a clown. They didn't know whether to promote him into the decision-making circle ... or whether to fire him. He followed no company rules, arrived at the executive offices according to his own schedule, but then sometimes confounded them all by working all night and miraculously pulling them out of one investment fiasco after another.

While the red-faced NIH executive whispered hoarsely in my ear, I overheard Ferdinando expounding his life theories to the other company officer who was more interested in peering down Giulia's low-cut blouse.

"Life is not actually determined by a series of turning points but by a process of gradual disintegration caused by the constant, day-to-day body blows like those of the boxer methodically working on his opponent's body preparing him for the big blow that inevitably comes, the one people remember as the knockout punch ... the punch we have to be prepared for and can later blame our failures on." I had to hold myself in rein not to interrupt for I knew he was twisting a Scott Fitzgerald quote to suit his own purposes.

Yet after that dinner and after his fall from the wall, my friend Ferdinando changed. For a week or so he seemed to walk normally, and evenings he still kicked the soccer ball around with ten-year old Dario out on the lumpy field opposite our houses. But then, gradually, as if suffering under the body work of his imaginary boxing opponent, he began favoring his left leg and blaming knee pains on both the lumps and holes in our field and on his mythical jump from the wall to save his kitten. Finally the pain became so severe that Antonia was able to convince him to see an orthopedist who, despite Ferdinando's terror of both needles and doctors, gave him a shot of cortisone.

Ferdinando came home that day and again played soccer with Dario, ran up and down the lumpy field opposite our houses and repeated that his jump was not the knockout punch it had seemed.

Things seemed to have returned to normal. Until two months later, the limp reappeared, the pain returned and the doctor gave him another shot which Ferdinando afterwards ruled was the very last. In any case this time it had no effect whatsoever.

The evening after the orthopedist prescribed a CAT scan, Ferdinando and I shared a bottle of Brunello which he had me bring up from his well-stocked wine cellar. After we were well into a second bottle, I noticed the tears in my friend's eyes, when he lamented that "*the natural state of the sentient adult is a qualified unhappiness*."

"Spinoza?" I, the writer, hazarded.

"F. Scott Fitzgerald!" he said triumphantly despite his tears.

As everyone knows it rarely snows in Rome. In normal years, at the very most a few flakes flutter from the sky to the delight of children and adults alike. If one inch of the white mantle falls during the night people break out sleds or even skis the next morning and head for the hilly parks while parents make snapshots of their children tumbling and frolicking in the wondrous white powder. Unexpectedly—and taking expert meteorologists by surprise—the snowfall that year turned out to be the biggest in popular memory. Moreover, it was the latest snowfall recorded in the annals of the capital city: the first flakes began to fall during the first week of April when usually the tourist Easter boom is underway and Palm Sunday was only a week away. As the size of the flakes and the velocity of their descent to Earth augmented, what struck Rome that year became a blizzard. Because of the unusual cold and Rome's lack of proper snow clearing equipment, the snow stuck on city streets, quickly turned to white ice and Rome looked like it might have in the Dark Ages.

In the suburbs where we live snow stood at a good eighteen inches in places and seemed to want to remain throughout the Easter season. Hotels emptied and restaurants closed for lack of customers and employees alike. Schools closed earlier than usual for the long Easter holidays. Transportation was at a standstill. City fathers issued warnings to citizens to stay indoors. Food shortage threatened. Normal civic life came to a halt.

During the ten days of the crisis, Antonia often brought her well-booted children to our house where she and Giulia passed their time. Ferdinando and I sat in his study and drank, chiefly from his red wine stock. While he limped around the study, through the parlors and to the kitchen for cheeses, I trudged up and down the cellar stairs fetching drinking supplies. He didn't care a whit about the blizzard and if not for Antonia's complaints he would have been quite happy with the situation. He lit a fire in the little used fireplace. We pulled our chairs near. While he drank freely Ferdinando talked as he never had before, spontaneously spilling out his innermost self.

"What melancholy, eh?" he said at one moment, a pleased look in his eyes. "Like nostalgia. Like the nostalgia you feel even for a place you've never been or might never see in your life. For me it's not only the kind of nostalgia and melancholy that this winter weather creates.

Our local train rounding the curve from La Storta in the night, its headlight sweeping majestically around the bend, makes my heart stop. And I'm saddened by the matted yellow lights from La Storta village there on the hill. The things on my mind seem to be far from the things others think. At times I feel strange, as if I knew things others do not and also at times as if I knew no one else on earth. My isolation is that of a person sharing the same space and time with others but in which each person is ultimately alone but in which part of you can still recognize the others."

"Maybe everyone desires that treasure of isolation, I mean, of total alienation," I said, interrupting his reverie ... "Maybe that's what real wealth is. Maybe everyone from time to time experiences that alienation from others … and oneself."

He ignored my remark and stared dreamily into the fire. "Like I say, you have to do something to make up a life. Maybe you just dream a life. Like history, life has its own rhythm, its own mysterious measures. Life makes its own demands, tempting and deceptive. Make-believe, too, is a way of life. Like my dreams. All my life I've had a rich dream life. I can pass from one dream to another or postpone it and continue later or sometimes repeat a particularly pleasant or rewarding dream. I can manipulate my dreams so that they are truly part of my life. Maybe I confuse dreams with fantasy. Why, you wonder, why all these dreams and make-believe? When I was a boy, dreams and make-believe were my safety net. Escape. Consider a moment yourself. Don't you think that everyone has to have an escape route?

"I've always walked a tightrope like over an abyss. Or on a razor's edge. That requires courage. Or naiveté. Forever on the verge of becoming extraordinary. Yes, extraordinary! Just before I again pull back toward the center. Fearful of taking the final step, I sigh and regretfully rejoin the ranks of the ordinary. And become … uh, uh, residential. That's the word I wanted. The post-risk disappointment then is so much the greater because I've always known that I am extraordinary. Who doesn't secretly consider himself extraordinary? You must admit that in your heart of hearts you believe you are extraordinary. If not, why live? I believe that each of us is unique. I hold that knowledge fast in my interior world of make-believe. In my dreams.

"Secretly vain, publicly humble, that's me! Yet to specify in my favor: humble in my vanity, vain in my humility. You see what I mean? The exception on one hand, one of the underdogs on the other. That's one of the reasons I love small countries. You can hold them in your grasp. You can encompass an entire society. Holland! Now that would be a country for me. Just the right size."

But that brief sojourn in paradise ended as soon as the thaw began and traffic began to move, trains began running and normalization was on the way, That was the moment Antonia broke the news that she was taking the children for a vacation to her parents' home on Lake Como in north Italy where it had not snowed at all.

The day after she and the children left Ferdinando was able to return to his job where he learned that in the meantime he had been "resigned".

I must say his reaction to his firing was most strange: he was neither upset nor happy; he was perplexed. It had been his first and only job and he had not even suspected he was under fire. He had sincerely believed that he was indispensable even though he admitted he didn't understand actuarial tables.

A generous bonus equal to more than a few years' salary, plus his stock options and various benefits actually left him a rather wealthy man. It was more the 'misunderstanding' of just what his position had been that disturbed him. Philosophically he described his old relationship with NIH with a proverb: "*Il gioco é bello se dura poco*." Fun games are great if they don't last too long.

He summed up his revised personal philosophy with another of his famous Fitzgerald quotes: "*A man does not recover from such jolts—he becomes a different person and, eventually, the new person finds new things to care about.*" I didn't exactly accuse him of lying but I saw that he grasped what I was thinking.

The snow and ice vanished in late April. May rains eliminated all vestiges of the blizzard and announced a return to normality. A June heat wave filled the local beaches with overjoyed Romans who had quickly deleted from memory the past Easter season that they would never again experience in their lives. Cosmic order had been restored.

But Ferdinando's life was one of total disorder: he now walked with the aid of a sturdy Sardinian shepherd's cane and after CAT scans showed serious lesions and torn meniscus in both knees he had finally agreed to operations. Moreover, Antonia and Chiara and Dario did not return from Lake Como. Ferdinando said they would most likely spend the summer on the mountain lake.

Evenings when he had dinner with us and he brought his ever ready wine, it was apparent to Giulia and me that his was a case of another of the proverbs he loved: *fare buon viso a cattiva sorte,* that is, make the best of a bad bargain, for he missed his family, his job and soccer play with the kids on the lumpy field.

Meanwhile he gave up his option on a nearby huge villa overlooking the plain reaching to the sea that had depended on his expected promotion with NIH. Now, faced with the new reality, he heard from Antonia that they would remain in Como for the next school year where she had a found an excellent private English school which they had both desired for their children.

Ferdinando simply did not know what to do with his time. His house seemed bigger and bigger, the gardens and yards a headache to maintain. And his wine supply was dwindling rapidly considering all his free time spent together with the red.

After dinner one evening we lingered over our wine. Dinner had been marked by long silences during which each of us seemed absorbed in his own thoughts.

After Giulia retired, Ferdinando insisted we open what I knew was his last bottle of Brunello and, barring a miracle, it would be the last. A September rain beat against the windows of the darkened dining room. Giulia had lit a candle which was burning low. Dolcezza slept curled up on Ferdinando's lap.

"She looks like she's in heaven," I remarked.

"Feline heaven," Ferdinando said. "She's just hoping nothing disturbs her peace."

"Nothing darker or more intimate than a rainy September night," I said. "When the great heat has ended but the cold has not yet arrived. I think it's the sudden intense darkness that makes it seem like the middle of the night."

"*In a real dark night of the soul it is always three o'clock in the morning*," Ferdinando murmured. "F. Scott Fitzgerald."

"What do you mean, my friend?"

"I mean to say that everything is so blinding that we see only blackness. Now I understand what I was blind to before."

"Before what?"

"Well, before my jump from the wall."

"You mean your fall … from the wall."

"My jump from the wall for Dolcezza here," he said, scratching the tiny kitten gently behind her ears. "And before the snowfall."

"The blizzard, you mean."

"The snowfall and my jump! Giacomo, will you please stop quibbling about terms, drink your wine and listen to me."

"OK! It's your wine. Shoot."

"There are two kinds of human psychology to keep in mind, my friend. First, the voluntary blindness to reality—like that of many people—in which you simply reject the facts right before you … as I did at NIH. The facts that disturb your comfort and ease. I didn't want to see that my relationship there was shaky and I, vulnerable. Secondly, there's the law of conformity which demands that you be like everyone else in order to be accepted by your milieu and that your thinking be consensual with the rest. That way of thinking is what is so terrifying to me. Those two psychologies together shape the great majority. So in that condition how can your own individuality come shining through? You tell me! We all experience that from day to day with our family, our friends and colleagues."

Like a chemist I poured equal portions of the last drops of our last Brunello about which we had once been so careless, pushed Ferdinando his glass, and raised mine to touch his.

"But now, Giacomo," he said touching my glass with a loud, almost joyous clink, "I feel outside of all that."

The Bösendorfer And Kafka's Long Lost Letter

1.

"You know, you have the best hands in the world," Matthew said, nuzzling her enticing bare shoulder lifting and moving so rhythmically up and down, up and down, as she stroked the romantic high keys of the Chopin sonata. After all, he thought, I'm an expert on the innate expertise of those hands. He imagined his body stretched out along the keyboard and as she ran her long fingers with her Calypso-like pink nails over the white keys and from time to time teased the blacks with furtive caresses he fewlt her sensual touch as if on himself. That wanton woman! he thought. She thrives on the suggestive with her sudden dips into the libertine. Matthew took her piano playing personally; he perceived her emphasis on Chopin's high notes like an irrefutable invitation. And spontaneously he kissed her right ear in acceptance.

"You should know," she said, reacting to his ear kiss in her usual sensual manner: her face flushed and with an audible little sigh she continued to tickle the keys while pressing her face hard against his. "And yours aren't bad either," she added in a husky voice.

Though she was called *petite*, Laura was actually tallish for an Italian woman, slim and with the perfect female protrusions in all the right places, and, Matthew believed, she had the sexiest hands and legs south of the Alps. "Just the way you react and say such things makes me … uh, makes me want to use the wide expanses of the top of this famous pianoforte for all those wonderful things we appreciate."

Physically, Matthew was nothing special, only slightly taller than his wife, neither slim nor robust, neither skinny nor muscular. But in Laura's words his *culo* was classical. She said his derrière was much more beautiful than that of Michelangelo's *Davide* sculpture which she dragged him to visit each time they were in Florence. All she had to do was say the word *culo* in her sinful way and his sham timidity vanished. Matthew and Laura spoke the same body language.

"I don't get you," Laura said, purposefully in her innocent mode. "What do you have in mind?"

"You know what I mean, dream lady. Us! On top of this would be Bösendorfer."

"Matthew, your words are ab-so-lute-ly sacrilegious … what you have in mind doing on top of the world's most sacred piano is ... is just *obscene*." Obscene was another of her favorite words: pronounced by Laura it meant everything that was vaguely licentious and thus desirable.

"Pianos! The Bösendorfer! You never talk so sanctimoniously about the Davide sculpture, after all one of the world's most admired works of art. But you speak of his 'perfectly beautiful behind' as if in a bordello. So it's the Bösendorfer for us, Laura love."

"Matthew!"

And so it went, their playfully debauched, love-filled vacation language in the shadow of the great Bösendorfer. Funny words were transformed into innuendo. Ordinary events became mysteries. Yet somehow the two-hundred and ninety centimeter long grand piano that had looked terrifyingly huge in the display room seemed to Matthew suspiciously small in the immense space of their vacation apartment ... and darker in color than he recalled. So either the leasing agency's display room was too small and poorly illuminated to accommodate the Bösendorfer Imperial 290 or the agency had sent them a fake. Still, its identification was inscribed under the keyboard lid: Bösendorfer. And it did have those nine extra keys in the bass part, all colored black, as the leasor recalled so that pianists could play on it Bach's works for the organ. Which was unimportant to them since Laura didn't play Bach and Matthew couldn't bear his organ stuff anyway. Odd though that Laura—who hadn't insisted on a Bösendorfer—hadn't noticed any disparities of sound. Why, she would've been just as happy with an upright. But he'd wanted for her the Bösendorfer 290, the king of pianos. It seemed proper for the 1920 atmosphere pervading Merano.

On the other hand, she hadn't seemed to notice the strangeness he'd felt the moment they stepped into the luxury apartment they'd taken for the Merano summer season. Meran, former resort of the Austro-Hungarian Empire; Italianized Merano, summer-winter resort of its new state, Italy. Like stepping back in time into a kind of twilight zone that in his ignorance about time he'd believed over and done. For today different wars were being fought and different plagues ravishing the land and the people. Like a return to the future. For 1920 hung in the air: as if the Great War had just been fought and the Spanish flu was killing the last millions and chic women were wearing Flapper cloche hats. Laura at the Bösendorfer seemed to symbolize those times.

Matthew saw mysteries everywhere. He was an investigator … of the unimportant, his wife teased. Not seeing the reality of the events happening in the period in which you live, he thought, was like trying to read a story but not even understanding the words in the text. And odd things were happening here. Little things. Puzzling things. Oh, those little things of life. Like the elevator that didn't stop at the third floor. Bizarre. A real mystery. Nothing to do with 1920 but it reminded him of the time his magazine sent him to Moscow for a story and his hotel had no seventh floor. As if the architect had simply forgotten it. Local people later explained the situation: unmentionable people occupied that floor. Publicly it didn't exist. But it did. And people knew. Now here in Merano there wasn't even a number 3 button in the elevator for the floor that existed just under them; they could see the number 3 written on the door when they passed it several times a day. The third floor was there, the space was there … but no call button, no stop, no people. So did it really exist?

Or no less puzzling: the three tall dogs as if from other times and their little Terrier companion confined in the penthouse above them for at least twenty-two hours a day. Russian Borzois, he believed, and a short-haired Yorkshire terrier, canine prisoners that never but never made the slightest sound whatsoever in the apartment. No barks, growls, whimpers. Nothing. Sometimes he fantasized that they were not really dogs at all, but some otherworldly creatures. Rare today, Borzois were popular and chic in the 1920s art deco aesthetic. Still, the strangest of all was that while he was so affected by mysterious events and people and objects, his wife never took notice of the inexplicable phenomena going on around them. Matthew, as insecure as he was curious, constantly perceived a dizzying swirl of mystery rising in their lives, the objects that refused to remain inanimate, places and things coming and going, all the unknown factors uniting with the apparent intention of engulfing them in the web of the uncertainties of things and time that refused to remain constant.

When Laura asked why everything stirred such emotions in him, he blushed and said that he needed his emotions ... just as much as they needed him. He later wondered why he said that. But no wonder, he thought. In the words of the poet Sharma the very search for a meaning in life is like discovering music in commotion or salt in the sand or water in parched land.

2.

Their summer vacation this year of 2020 was exceptional. The whole 2020 was uncommon, sensations of the end of an epoch infecting the very air and making people in conservative Merano unusually carefree in the festive 1920 stage setting. In their reconstruct the Spanish flu had finally ended after its catastrophic passage through the world and Meran's era of glory lived on. Back in the future of 2020 the statistical curve of the virus pandemic was beginning to descend farther south down the peninsula but the fever had never even begun in this Alpine resort. Here you felt apart from the main, truly an island, in a different world and time. Time lost its linearity; time zigzagged crazily. People two hundred kilometers to the south were in 2020 quarantine while people of Merano were instead celebrating the centennial anniversary of Franz Kafka's stay in their city from April to June of 1920. The twilight era of one hundred years ago being relived. The whole year was marked by exhibits and lectures and organized visits to Kafka's Meran, as the small Spa city in this ethnic German territory of the Austro-Hungarian Empire was designated when Kafka lived here to heal his lungs. The acclaimed Meran air didn't improve his health, Kafka later claimed, so he spent his time writing love letters to Milena Jesenskà in Vienna, letters destined to become his famous book, *Letters To Milena*.

This morning, with such mysteries, suppositions and emotions stirring his psyche—if the psyche even exists, Matthew thought—he had been observing Laura at the putative Bösendorfer, marveling at the assuredness and appeal her upright figure exuded. Though her self-assurance underlined his lack of it, he nonetheless loved the way she sat at the piano, so straight, her posture perfect, and at the same time so relaxed and easy in her element, her light eyes now glistening in the rays of the mid-morning sunlight as the pink disk rose from behind the hovering mountains rising to the east. He contemplated those extra nine bass keys on the piano which the agency man had so vaunted. Laura never used them. Practically nobody does ... except a few specialists who insist on playing Bach organ music on a Bösendorfer piano. Who in their right mind would want to be a specialist on Bach organ music for the piano? Matthew disliked specialists intensely; his ideal was the Renaissance creator. Still, something in that piano was amiss; he had to return to that agency and clarify the Bösendorfer affair.

While Laura played Chopin, Matthew pranced across the wide hardwood spaces to one of the great windows overlooking nature's spectacle that after two days he had come to love at any hour. On the one side lay wide green fields bordered by coniferous forests that continued to the foot of the mountain leading to the peak of the *Kuhleiten* they planned to climb. On the other side, a lake beyond which more mountains in the direction of Austria and his father's Germany. They were surrounded by nature's many inexplicable manifestations. He was ruminating about the contrast between the outside world of nature and the pianos and the art inside when he heard again the same brouhaha down in the gardens: first the furious barking and then the emergence of the three sleek tall dogs—most definitely Russian Borzois—followed by the short-haired Terrier, its short legs pumping to keep up with the others racing toward some obscure objective outside Matthew's vision. Each time the doorman took them out, the same scene was repeated. Twice a day: the four dogs barking and yelping raced around blindly just to give vent to their wild nature so totally pent-up all those hours in their penthouse penitentiary.

"You know, Laura, there's something peculiar about this piano," he began, starting the trek back cross the room. Suddenly he stopped, turned toward the wall and said, "Ciao, Egon!" to the portrait of his favorite painter, Egon Schiele. Curious, he mused, that we have his portrait but not one of his works. Laura probably had it put there. How thoughtful of her. He touched it reverently, always saddened because he died so young … of the Spanish flu. Flu a century ago, flu-like Covid-19. He'd long wondered if Egon was madman or saint? Well, whatever, he was pure genius.

"So, Laura I've decided to write a story within the story, the story of this mysterious Bösendorfer. Of course my real story is about Kafka, seeing he's what brought us here in the first place. Hmm! Well, I googled it, the Bösendorfer, I mean, and learned a lot of interesting stuff. Things that make that so-called musical instrument agency in Bolzano look phony. Why, that may not be a real Bösendorfer at all. At least not one made by the Bösendorfer Klavierfabrik Gmbh in Vienna. Laura, this piano may just be dead wood, a beautiful piece of furniture but without anything super musical inside it. Without a soul. Yet, now that I think of it, this piano may have an evil soul: it may contain somewhere in its chords a complex surveillance instrument that intercepts top secret data of industrial espionage in our country and in Austria and Switzerland and Germany, too. A four-country instrument. Only God knows the things they invent these days."

"Oh, for heaven's sake, Matthew! We just got here and you're already off on another of your imaginative trips into that other world you live in ... always busy picking up the broken pieces of something or other." Laura had observed her obsessed husband from the moment he'd arrived at the great window overlooking the fields and the forests and the mountains and stood there on purpose, she thought, flexing his beautiful derrière while he listened to the barking of the dogs, his head nodding as if in agreement with some mad ideas churning in his mind. She knew he would re-tell his act of simply taking a look out the window as some great adventure over there on the other side of the immensity of this gigantic space, as he described the room.

Matthew said: "Well, my love, if you can tear yourself away from the Bösendorfer we can set out as planned on our Kafka In Meran Day. The sun is shining, the air fresh, and we're in no rush. I thought a glance at the Grand Hotel Emma where Kafka only stayed a few days—too expensive for the poor sick man—before moving to the Pension Ottoburg where he wrote those amazing love letters. I'll quote from some of them in my article. And on our way over to Lower Maia to see the Ottoburg we can walk along the Passirio River on the Passerpromenade as it's called in German. I understand that the villa looks just as it did as a guest house … one hundred years ago, mind you."

3.

"Oh, *per l'amor di Dio*, Matthew, what are you smirking about?" Laura said, squirming around in the front row seat in the City Theater and whispering that she couldn't wait to get back to the piano. Some ideas had occurred to her while waiting for the Professor to speak. "We've done everything according to what you keep calling *our* plan. I just wanted to play my piano. But no, I had to come with you on this Kafka chase. We saw the school that was once the Grand Hotel Emma… back in the Belle Epoch, all a century ago. We … "

"Laura, my great love, we're about to hear the Munich Professor Zecke speak of the greatest writer of that period, Franz Kafka."

"And as you said registered at the hotel as 'Herr Doktor Kafka, employee from Prague.' Matthew, was Kafka not the one who became a bug and wrote a book about it?"

"Yes, Laura, The Metamorphosis. *Die Verwandlung*. His protagonist becomes a cockroach … by the way prompting the supposition that he was schizoid. Anyway Laura, you have to stop this! One sacrilege after the other. Please! You just never know about an artist. I read that effeminate Chopin hated people in general, but he still wrote beautiful music." Matthew was struck by the capability of artists to adapt to the customs of those diverse peoples among whom they happen to live. Uncertain as to whether that mental characteristic merited reproach or praise, he thought it proof of the artist's incredible flexibility and his thought so sensibly pure that he could forgive even evil when he sees its necessity or the impossibility of its elimination.

"Matthew, *Tesoro*, didn't you say that this alleged professor's name, Zecke, means 'tick". Oh Dio! So we're here to listen to Doctor Tick speak about cockroaches."

"Well, yes. But the subject of that novel is important, nothing to do with the meaning of names. You know, how in modern society we're alienated one from the other... Alienation, Laura, a sign of the times."

"Like you from me, eh? Still there seems to be too much ado here about insects. Well, I don't speak the professor's German and I'm alienated from the rest of you here ... even from you ... you and your German father and German schools. But cockroaches? No, Matthew, this is just too much. Cockroaches!" she muttered, standing up noisily right under the nose of the startled speaker just as he stepped onto the stage. "See you later, alligator! You'll find me at my Bösendorfer."

4.

There was nothing Kafkaesque about Herr Doktor Professor Mattäus Zecke. Much younger than Matthew had imagined him, Zecke was dressed in a dark brown cardigan and blue jeans, had long hair and a hippie look about him. Holding a microphone in one hand and sheets of notes in the other, he stood near the edge of the stage looking straight down at Matthew in front row center.

"*Also, Meraner Freunde* ... So, Meran friends, Kafka specialists have long believed there is a missing Kafka letter ... and that that letter is still somewhere here in the Meran where he spent his three sleepless months that we're celebrating today ... writing letters to Milena. But what letters!"

Aware that his opening was unusual, Zecke stopped, lowered the mic and looked down at Matthew as if waiting for his reaction. Matthew nodded knowingly and gazed back straight into the young professor's eyes, somewhat surprised at his North German accent. He'd expected the young professor was from Munich like his own father. So that he would speak like local people here. But he sounded like a Berliner. So different from local Tyroleans. Different in mentality. Zecke had just confirmed that peculiar things were indeed taking place here in the Alpine *Meraner Luft*. In the air of Meran. Much more than cloche hats.

"Well, Ladies and Gentlemen, I have found that missing letter!"

"What!" Matthew exclaimed, leaping to his feet, his phone, notebook and pen clattering on the hardwood floor just under Zecke's eyes.

"Seems to run in the family," the speaker said, leaning toward to Mathew collecting his stuff while people in the front rows guffawed.

"Strange things are going on everywhere," he answered, grinning sheepishly up at Zecke. "Just have to get used to them."

After an embarrassed Matthew got re-settled in his seat, Zecke started over: "In 1920, Franz Kafka and Milena Jesenská began a love affair … at first through letters. Now you all know Kafka the great writer but who was Milena? Well, Milena was a twenty-three year old journalist and aspiring writer and translator who lived in Vienna in a crumbling marriage. An astute young woman, she recognized Kafka's genius long before others did. Despite the distance and despite the insurmountable blocks between German-writing Kafka in Prague and Czech-writing Milena in Vienna, the two developed an intense and intimate relationship. In their letters they literally stripped their bourgeois identities and bared their souls. The correspondence started when Milena wrote to Kafka asking for permission to translate his short story 'The Stoker' from German to Czech. That request quickly turned into a series of passionate and profound letters that Milena and Franz exchanged from March to December 1920. Kafka wrote daily, often several times a day. He told her to write every day, too, even if just one word, *'without which I would suffer terribly.'* He suffered on *letterless* days. Their letters are also linguistically interesting; Kafka wrote his letters in German—even though he was fluent in Czech—while Milena wrote in her Czech mother tongue.

"I think that at some point his soul began to suffer, too. He wrote of his soul more than once. Now the soul was not a subject many critics have attributed to Kafka's concerns. But some have. One day in June he asked Milena to react to his soul sickness. But got no answer. So he wrote another letter asking about the one dispatched the day before ... but the letter of the day before never arrived. It never arrived because it never left Meran. It has been here all these one hundred years.

"Kafka wrote Milena about his anxieties, fears, loneliness; his published letters reveal the extent of his anguish caused by Milena, the sleepless nights, and the futile situation of their love. Milena haunted his thoughts. She was his 'savior'. Passionate, vivacious and courageous, Milena suffered greatly because of him, as Kafka said himself: *Do you know, darling? When you became involved with others you quite possibly step down a level or two, but if you become involved with me, you will be throwing yourself into the abyss.* She knew that herself, and yet she chose to sink because lust for life was part of her personality, and pain and rapture go hand in hand. Dostoyevsky was her favorite writer who confirms the propensity towards pain typical of Slavic women as was Milena. The Slavic soul is a deep and dark place that one cannot wander into out of mere curiosity. Two such dark souls would have trouble living a simple life together. Their relationship was hot and cold; intense at one moment because their minds were alike, then alienated one from the other by distance. When she yearned to see him in Vienna, he was reluctant; when he wanted her to divorce her husband and come live with him, she wasn't keen to do so.

"Yet though they were different in age and personality, no other woman entranced Kafka so much, and despite the abrupt end of their passionate correspondence, I think Milena was just what he needed. Still, Kafka felt the age difference. He wrote and I quote: '*It took some time before I finally understood why your last letter was so cheerful; I constantly forget the fact that you're so young, maybe not even 25, maybe just 23. I am 37, almost 38, older by a whole short generation, almost white-haired from all the cold nights and headaches.*' He wrote: '*You see, the peaceful letters are the ones that make me happy.*'"

Zecke finally explained the missing letter. "I found it", he said reaching into the pocket of his jeans and pulling out a pocket watch, "exactly ninety minutes ago. This is what happened: Kafka apparently gave his letter to Milena to the concierge-handyman at the Ottoburg for posting —the twenty-two year old already known as 'Old Hansli'. But precisely that morning there was an unprecedented deluge in Meran. The waters of the Passer River rose, streets and houses were flooded. In short, Meran friends, when many days later the rains ceased and the flood waters relented, the letter was forgotten. It was never mailed. Many years then passed. World War Two came and went. On his death in 1980, Hansli's son Rainer who'd worked his way up from chasseur to the concierge position at the prestigious Belle Epoque Hotel Europe Splendid found the letter among his father's papers in a basket in his attic. Unaware of its historical significance the today ninety-year old Rainer had left it in that same basket. I found it there!"

After Zecke finished speaking, Matthew hung around until the nimble professor jumped down from the stage where he stopped him. There was something fishy about the story of the letter. These Tyroleans like to play games. They love Bavarians of south Germany but Berliners are not among their favorites. Maybe Zecke hadn't understood the ex-concierge. Or maybe the concierge was playing tricks on a gullible Prussian.

"I say, Zecke … uh, Professor, do you have a moment? I'm, er, a reporter, working on a story about Kafka in Meran."

"A moment, yes. What can I do for you?"

"The letter of course. I would very much like to get a copy of it."

"Well, you can understand it is a great find for a scholar so …"

"Zecke, are you confident of the letter's authenticity? Like the handwriting? Is it a real letter, properly dated as were all Kafka's letters to Milena? And the envelope, is it, uh, of the period of one hundred years ago? You know, stuff like that."

"Look, as I said, I just found it. But I will get experts to examine it and authenticate it. Certainly I don't intend going down in literary history as the sponsor of a falsified letter of Franz Kafka."

"Well, I think you should know that these Tyroleans like to joke around. *Das Leben ist nur ein Scherz,* they sing. Life is only a joke. And, well, if a Prussian is the butt of a Tyrolean game, then …"

"Oh, I'm not a Prussian. I'm just from the North … from a village between Hamburg and Berlin."

"But didn't you find it strange that a long lost letter from one of last century's major writers was just lying there in a basket waiting for you … and after one hundred years and a world war and their land becoming Italian? Anyway, can I get a copy?"

"We'll see. But only after I get back to Berlin and decide how to handle this delicate affair. Just leave your address with my secretary over there," he said, pointing at a sexy dark-haired young woman sitting on a straight chair facing the auditorium, her legs dangerously apart.

Matthew didn't dare. He handed Zecke his card.

5.

The concierge at the Hotel Splendid was honored to give the Herr Doktor Journalist, that is, Matthew, his predecessor's address, a big house a few blocks away along the banks of the Passirio, the river's Italianized name. Though Franz Thomas Rainer Müller—an important citizen of Merano—was named for Thomas Mann, Rainer Maria Rilke and Franz Kafka—all of whom former visitors to Meran—everybody called him Franzi. For effect, Matthew imitated his own father's Munich accent to inquire about the lost Kafka letter joke.

"*Ach, das war ja nur ein Scherz.*" The ex-concierge snickered and slapped one hand into the other. "Just a joke and the Prussian fell for it. *Ach*, they're so gullible! They once fell for a crazy stupid failure of a painter, too."

"Well, the Kafka letter is a pretty serious matter … for all of Meran."

"And so was that mean Austrian … for the whole world."

"Well, Franz Thomas Rainer, you're a very perspicacious man, just as you should be with all those wonderful names!," Matthew said in genuine admiration. "So okay, it was a joke on the Prussian. And a joke is a joke. Still, may I ask if you know anything about pianos? I saw a grand piano in the lobby of your former hotel. Quite beautiful."

"Ja ja, I myself had it installed there years ago. My nephew rents pianos over in Bolzano. Oh, he told me he leased a Bösendorfer to some vacationer here." The ex-concierge smiled his playful old man's smile. "Is that vacationer you?"

"*Ja, richtig*, and my wife loves it. But you know, Franzi, there's something funny about it. Don't know what it is. That piano has nine extra keys. They're colored black. But my wife never uses them. Chopin and all, you know. But I tried each of them out, just to hear the sound. Deep bass sounds. But one key, the one in the middle of the black nine, just goes 'plunk'. No sound. Something strange about that piano, the Bösendorfer … the King of Pianos or not."

Franzi was now all grins and snickers and slapping his hands on his legs as if to dance a Tyrolean *Schuhplattler*. "Ah ha, then maybe you know more than you think you know. Some things you just have to open up and take a good look inside. Like a surgeon does when he looks around inside an open stomach. Like when guests at my hotel were hospitalized—or even died—and we had to open their suitcases for some reason. *Mein Herr*, the things we found inside! Surprising finds. Everything from high-powered guns to manuscripts to enough barbiturates to kill a horse."

6.

Musing that concierges were among the best-informed people of the world, Matthew made his way back to their apartment. The bizarre atmosphere not only still reigned; it had intensified. But he couldn't fathom why he felt that. On his approach through the condominium's gardens, he stopped to watch the three tall Borzois and the little Terrier race past, their heads lifted toward the orange-colored heavens and the sun-lit mountains to the East and barking out of pure joy at their existence and their participation in the spectacle of nature around them. Where else in the world will I ever witness again such an extravaganza of the Earth, in this very moment threatened by mankind and defended only by its own eternal nature? With the dogs and the sunset in mind, on the elevator he hardly took notice of the absurd missing third floor.

He found Laura where she promised to be: at the Bösendorfer Imperial 290 and playing her beloved Chopin. She was wearing a Flapper-girl cloche. Well, so that's where we are, he thought. This bewildering story started in an unusual way right here at this piano that I always found strange, and now events, people, objects and history seem to be coming to a head in an unusual way, again at this Bösendorfer Imperial 290 … all happening according to the natural order of things. For a moment he admired his wife whose hands ran up and down the keyboard so freely, but his major attention was fixed on those nine darkened bass keys she ignored. The Bösendorfer itself occupied his inner vision and most of his conscious mind.

"Laura, my heartbeat," he began absently, "did you know that a Bösendorfer piano was thrown off the *Queen Elizabeth II* into the ocean during the Falkland Islands conflict in 1982 to make room for helicopters."

"For heaven's sake, Matthew!"

"Just thought you'd like to know that," he said vaguely, peering into the innards of the Bösendorfer as if into its very soul. Kafka thinking, he realized. And, for the first time he perceived this piano as a genuine Imperial 290. Peering into its secrets, he traced the chords into the dark left corner of the mammoth instrument ... and there it was, just as Franzi the concierge had hinted: a tightly bound packet hidden by a piece of the spruce or beech or maple of the grand piano. Spontaneously he thrust his hand in and yanked the packet loose, and let out a whoop:

"Got it. Now Laura, try that fifth black key!

"Dong!"

"Again, Laura. Again!"

"Dong, dong, dong, dong, dong."

"Now to read the real lost letter," he said, his mounting excitement infecting also Laura. "Or is it like the piano a fake?" he said, his eyes fixed on Laura's. "Somehow I've never believed the piano is a real Bösendorfer anyway."

They opened the only slightly dusty package and there before them on the white and black keyboard lay a two-page letter. Immediately he checked the signature: *Franz.* The envelope was addressed to Frau Milena Jesenska. Matthew translated aloud the opening lines: *"For one human being to love another, Rainer Maria Rilke* wrote, *is perhaps the most difficult of all our tasks ... the work for which all other work is but preparation."*

In the second paragraph Kafka, too, turned to the soul: *"The observer of the soul cannot penetrate into the soul, but there is doubtless a margin where he comes into contact with it. Recognition of this contact is the fact that even the soul does not know of itself. Hence it must remain unknown. That would be sad only if there were anything apart from the soul, but there is nothing else."*

"Laura, this doesn't sound like the rest of his letters to Milena, he …"

"It doesn't sound like the other letters because this was compiled by others, Matthew. And recently. These scraps of beautiful paper, this whole thing is a forgery. How do I know? Open your mind and look closely at the paper and the matching envelope. Don't you recognize it? This was not written one hundred years ago. Nor fifty years ago. Probably it was written recently. This is written on designer stationary, expensive, the kind used for luxury editions of important books. Look at the grain of the paper, the thickness, the weight. And see that tiny brown dot in the upper left corner? That's the mark of the Cavallini Company. I think I still have some of the stationary at home. So the number of false Kafka letters mounts. We now have two. How many do you think there can be?"

"Who knows, Laura, my treasure? But, as they say in German, Life is only a joke. *Das Leben ist nur ein Scherz."*

THE SCENT OF MAHAGONY

1.

At thirty-six years I'm on record as the youngest Operations Director in the history of the international cultural organization where I've worked for the last nine years. Now I'm not at all overjoyed about my promotion to this position, nor did I even aspire to the job because of the weighty character demands on the holder. But my wife insisted that the big salary increase outweighed those negative aspects, demands however that in times past have brought about the downfall of many others before me. In any case, I find my nomination as anomalous as a North Korean declaration of war on the US of A, the result of a combination of circumstances that should never have happened. So it was pure chance that I, Montgomery Morgan, the anti-bureaucrat personified, came to occupy such a rigid administrative job.

It happened like this: my predecessor and former boss fell into a weird sort of sleepy immobility, content to just sit at his beloved mahogany desk and sign papers. While I, his assistant, unknowingly had the instinct to strike out into the unexplored territories management desired. Yet, though my life now seems a Camelot to others, my career flight cannot resolve my painful existential problem: my daughter of two and a half years died eighteen months ago. An incurable organic allergy, the doctors claimed. But I doubt they really know. And whether they know or not, the thought that medical science might disprove their diagnosis is a perpetual torment like that of the dying man convinced of a future definitive cure of brain cancer, but too late to save him.

Since then, the months, weeks, days, hours of pain and disbelief have dragged past, during which only action for action's sake counts. Pain in the early morning, pain at night, and passing time marked by a contradictory inertia in my interior life. A time of empty but unfillable spaces and of unidentified voids, while my wife and I have become strangers to each other. In our separate sufferings our former love withered away like remnants of Marx's bourgeois state. And only I know that my seemingly tireless energy comes from my frantic attempts to fill the hole of *her* absence.

So, on the one hand, I feel I owe my truncated family the material benefits my new position brings … to compensate for what is missing; on the other hand, my asymmetrical public self parodies the nouveau rich I so despise, a life style which I believe is only a shadow side of my real self, a mimesis caused by my weakness of character. Yet, *it* is in me. And not even my wife is aware of the extent of my unceasing pain. That thing is in me, that monster, the *it* that taunts me that *she* will never come back ... as if she could if she only wanted to.

While those uncontainable fears nest in my interior life, overnight, it now seems, I became that other public person, living a sham life which I perceive as a black mark on my persona. While time has crept past, I've begun to wonder if what I now think of as my unfreedom of today actually did begin in the still obscure past that my psychiatrist harps on. In any case, I see my king's clothes, my privileges, and the prestige and power my new position brings as symbols of my slavery to an alien way of life.

Looking back, I can pinpoint as precisely as if under the electronic sights of a Russian R-38 ICBM the day, the hour, the very minute I became aware of the change in my public life: it was on the same day that the rains began. A hard constant rain, as unceasing as the rain during Noah's forty days and forty nights. Day and night, week after week, the rain fell on the city that thank heavens had the miraculous capacity of absorbing rather than accumulating on the surface what seemed all of the atmosphere's water.

That first day of the great rain, at precisely 15:15 hours, the personnel director, a trendy Parisian, pushed me through the door of a renowned Czech tailor, so classy that his studio facing onto a small park tucked away in the Old City was identified only with a small brass wall plaque with his name engraved in gray letters: *Cyril.* All that old Bohemian had to do was gander my sloppy dress. I must have looked unbearably bohemian to him. But the moment that cunning tailor-artist had me touch those Irish woolens I was as if transformed from hippy to bourgeois in one quick swipe … yet only a provisional digression, I believed. A temporary abandonment of the real me. I believe I knew—I had to know—my real life was a straight line.

Czech-made suits of Irish woolens with tasteful matching vests and cashmere topcoats and Italian sports cars. Signs of the times; the ugly symbols of my new life. And all the while, deep in my guts, I perceived the fear of the price I would have to pay. For though you may change, your core self remains. Something always remains. You are still you. Therefore the necessity of pinpointing the exact moments when the key events occur. Like the clock time when I stepped into the tailor's atelier: 15 hours and 15 minutes. But still, I hope for the chance to relive this period of my life and to try again and do better next time. I've come to understand why negative nostalgia exists: nostalgia for the bad moments, a longing to grasp the specific moments when you could have become someone better ... and did not. Sometimes I search again for those ugly moments in order to feel again the initial panic and perceive the regret, and wish I'd taken other paths.

Just after my nomination, the earth seemed to fall from under me. The change of offices became the emblem of the change taking place inside me: the giant move from the adjoining sub-office to the vastness of the thickly carpeted room with the great windows and antique furniture and the huge mahogany desk behind which I swore never to sit. Oh, it's not that splendid wood that I hate, the hard wood used in many lands to make furniture and boats and even the most delicate musical instruments, the brilliant reddish brown wood called in our languages: mahogany, mahogani, mogano, acajou, caoba, krasnoye derevo. It's that specific desk I detest. I pile books and papers on it to disguise it. I spread my precious maps across it to hide it. Bottled water stands near my faithful boom box. Dust and must accumulate on that desk among jackets and coats and caps, helter-skelter, sheaves of dusty notes of ideas waiting to be developed, old photographs, unread memos, and secret papers the *executive secretary* should file away in cabinets where they can fade and never be seen again. Oh, how I detest that title … as I detest the desk and the title: Executive Secretary. Is that woman really a secretary? Or management's spy? How can I ever be free here if my secretary is their spy?

On another ambiguous day I walked around the immense but still foreign room and stared out the window at the monotonously falling rain and wondered where it would all end. I spun around in the leather swivel chair, sat at the shiny conference table the cleaning women polish each morning, ran my fingers in circles over the surface as perfect as a homemade *marron glacé* and hated this office with the absurd mahogany desk where I feel as otherworldly as Kafka slipping out of his sanatorium and walking the streets of Meran in search of a Viennese *Konditorei* serving the perfect *Apfelstrudel*. Were I to occupy this office for a lifetime, I would always be a stranger in it. From the great window I stared at the hypnotic falling rain and perceived my old sense of loneliness enveloping me. The rain's descent seemed unusually slow, hesitant, jerky, like that of a glass-encased elevator sliding up and down its fixed path inside a crumbling shopping mall. I tried to isolate one individual raindrop and follow its fall to the surrounding roofs so much like the grey zinc sheet roofs of Paris until I felt I was truly elsewhere. I felt the vertigo.

Did my predecessor who became so piously pompous when he entered this same office never have the anarchic impulses that overcome me here in the proximity of the mahogany desk? No, he did not. He loved this office. He'd liked to ensconce himself behind the shiny wooden monster that he kept immaculate and barren; he would extend both arms over the smooth surface, his palms flat on the polished wood, his sleeves rolled up in two folds as precise as the sleeves of an SS officer's black uniform. The ritual seemed to reinforce his conviction that everything was under control. Then he would summon me or the executive secretary to ask about an obscure memo, or he would telephone the building superintendent to ask some banality about the proper office temperature. That man was never free, not for one moment of his life was he ever free. Oh, how I despise the murderous enslaving bureaucracy and their standard issue mahogany desks.

2.

Meanwhile the orgy began. Anything to kill the pain, I thought. I, Monty, trembled in terror. I suffered. Work by day, play by night. Women of the city. The loss of a child changes everything. An estranged wife, and I, a failure of a father. So what should I do? What could I do? I had to prove myself as never before.

I became aware I was living a reconstructed life. A new kind of life that I tried to relate to my renewed reality. Oh, I'd once believed I held everything in my hands. That my life was under control. But it all slipped away. Or perhaps I let it slip away. I don't know why. Out of cowardice? Or a lack of prudence? Or was it fear? The reality is I don't know what I'm most afraid of. I was never fearful. Not before. That's why I'm recounting this here. But at some point I became wary. About taking new steps. About speaking new words. Dostoevsky wrote something like that.

One night, months after it all began, I was walking along the riverfront street toward my car parked downriver from the apartment of a casual lady friend. It was past midnight. Traffic was light. The street lamps flickered in Noah's prodigious rain. Strangely, I felt at one with the indistinctness of the moment, my thoughts jagged and unhinged, darting wildly here and there, from time to time recalling her as I'd left her in the big room facing the rushing river. The magical river locked in a symbiotic relationship with the endless rain. Were they not the same thing? Same origin, same destination? For like the never-ending rain, there's something mystical about this narrow river rushing so arrogantly down from the mountains and gushing in a fury through the center of the big city. As if water were a divinity. A divinity shorn of signs of a heaven or a hell. A water god. Yet, strange things, inexplicable things, could happen along this river in the night under the unceasing charge from the heavens piercing even the homes of people who profess principles and morals, tenderness and truth, but still feel terror of the hereafter. It's the water, I know, that causes such thoughts.

I became conscious of a blinking light farther down the darkened river. At first, it was a mere spark, then round and flickering. I accelerated my pace, long strides in the rain, faster and faster. Ah hah, so that's it, I thought when the siren began, dah-dah, dah-dah, dah-dah. Faster, ever faster. But I got no closer to the now fiery sphere, nor to the siren. We seemed to form a fixed triangle: I, the fire, the siren, the three points. I leaning forward and pressing ahead in the rain, the fire and the dah-dah still the same distance from me and from each other.

Kids roasting sausages on the riverside, under Noah's rain? Hooligans setting fire to Roma shacks? I walked past my parked car and continued on down the river.

And all of a sudden the fire was real … and near. Brash voices blasted out from the opposite riverbank: 'Burn, burn, burn! Hey, you there! Throw that monster kid in the water. Yeah, there. Out into the deep part … out there … near the rocks.'

Screams. Cries. In Roma language. Big men wearing ski masks burning the Roma shacks. Nocturnal killers killing the Roma. Killing their people. Killing me. Like the rain and the river, I and the Roma of the same origin and with the same destination. Our bodies the selfsame sixty per cent water, each of us terrified of the threatening one hundred per cent. They, unreachable across the raging river; I, to them invisible on the opposite side; both of us in search of salvation from water.

Auden said that we are here on Earth to help others. But what could I do? I could do nothing. I wasn't afraid. I was a prisoner on the opposite bank from all the burning. Separated by the surging river and the falling rain, my thoughts as fragile as the Maginot Line uselessly defending Paris in '40'.

Then, all at once, the sirens fell silent. They'd given up. I was alone with the killers and the Roma maybe dying in the raging red reflections-flecked water. Annoyed at first, then fearfully, guiltily, I ran back to my car and drove off in the opposite direction; just not to see the masked killers (they had to be masked) and the burning shacks, nor hear the Roma screaming and the rushing river gurgling under the incessant rain. But in my mind's eye the embers of the extinguished fire continued to glow like airport runway beacons in the night; then gradually the screams grew weaker, and fell silent. But I knew the fire on the opposite riverbank and the screams in the night would return. I felt a mounting responsibility.

I drove around the city in the nocturnal downpour asking myself why I didn't try to help as Auden said we should. Am I a coward? I don't know. I've never been tested. Never even a physical test until tonight. But was this test valid? Did it count? Well, why should it not count? For what happened really happened. If I saw what I thought I was seeing, I *was* being tested. But who was testing me? Lord, Lord, I just happened to be there after a rendez-vous with a lady friend.

Love? Would love change anything? It can? It does? It changes everything? It's the emergency exit. Do you maybe mean that if I loved her, my unascertained cowardice would not count? Oh, yes, I agree, love counts for sure. But my love-making in the room looking over the gurgling river water cannot be related to my cowardice in the rain on the riverbank.

I keep using that word: cowardice. However, there are many degrees of cowardice. Synonyms such as cravenness and dastardliness seem far-fetched, spineless and banal. Timidity and wariness are only vaguely cowardly! I'm insecure but not timid. Most likely I'll never know if it was cowardice that blocked me on the riverside. Never know if I lost the chance of a lifetime.

Disclaimers come to mind: the fiery red was a fata morgana. Or if it *was* real, it was just kids having fun around a bonfire. And that dah-dah-dah-dah was normal urban noise. Or, it was all a figment to begin with, something about a triangle. My wild imagination. And my affliction.

3.

I drove aimlessly around the city. Where should the coward go? Home, to wife and children? Or off into the night to the one who would welcome me in her loving way? In any case, my hours no longer seemed unusual … not to friends and lovers. Street lights flashed past. Windshield wipers swished, back and forth, back and forth, tac tac tac, faster and faster, and I wondered where all the water came from. Back and forth I crossed bridges over the Stygian river, sped through yellowish urban tunnels, stared at the unbearable fixed red light atop the television tower and listened for the siren speaking its repetitive language.

Abruptly, I found myself parked in front of her house in the northern part of the city. The rain drummed on the car roof. I still smelled the fire. Could I go in to her, smelling of fear?

Nastya was not surprised. She's used to my hours. She says my life is surreal. Her arms went around me.

'I was waiting. I'm always waiting. Do you love me?'

'Of course. I'm here to love you,' I said, thinking: coward, coward, coward. Did I reek of the coward's fear?

Nastya was ecstatic. I was disgusted with me. Not because of the other woman. But because of the river fires and the Roma dying in the water on fire. Coward! I screamed to myself.

'Nastya, am I a coward?' I asked, later.

'Why? What have you done that was so cowardly?'

I told her about the river fires, the shacks burning, the Roma screaming, the siren singing. I had to tell somebody. 'I wasn't really afraid. Not much. Besides there was that raging water between us, looking like the River Styx. It's what I did *not* do. I didn't even cross the river. I didn't even try to save one single child, Nastya. I just came to you. Driving around in that mad rain I had the thought that cowardice and ignorance are linked. Sometimes you're just too ignorant to realize that you're a fearful coward … so you go on living your life thinking you're heroic.'

'Out there in the rain and the blinding lights your imagination distorts reality, Montgomery."

'It seemed real.'

'Our there you see things in a different way. You see events that never happen. Anyway, kids love to build bonfires. Especially on riverbanks … even in the rain. Didn't you know that? An Aryan rite.'

I leaned forward and looked at her closely. She looked heroic. I live again in Nastya. I live in the present tense my time with her. She looks taller in a long old-fashioned nightgown, her hair blonder than usual in the dimness of candle-light. Beautiful and sensual, but also homey ... reassuring me that everything will be all right.

'What? Kids around bonfires in the rain. No, I didn't know that. Just imagine, on the riverside in the rain.'

I think about kids for a while. I think about bonfires. I think about arks and reservoirs of water without end. But I don't see the kids and the bonfires in my mind. I'm unsure what I'm seeing.

'Nastya, I would stay for the night if you don't mind.' Why does she love me, the coward?

'I want you here. But don't you have to go home? At some hour?'

'Go back home? At some point you can't go back ... maybe never ever again. There's a point of no return. No. I can't go back. Above all, not tonight. Not after the fire on the riverbank … and all that water. Not after their screams and that dah-dah stronger and stronger … then fading in the night … so that I don't even know if it was real.'

'Oh, *Serdtze*, just ordinary city noises.'

'And to think I was once so free. All the freedom in the world. Then my unfreedom began. But then I don't think you can ever go back to the same old freedoms, can you?'

'I don't know, my heart. But recently I read a great writer who noted that we have to open our eyes and accept that real human life lies beyond hopelessness. And Montgomery, you know well that life's not always heroic. There's also tragedy … like yours.'

And so, willy-nilly a new kind of life began. Right here. In this apartment. On this square. Under the deluge, I fell in love. How could I've not loved her? Six months of a new form of hopelessness passed. In hopeful hopelessness.

4.

One morning I was sitting at the long conference table in my uninspiring office and wondering what would happen that day. In disgust I looked over the mayhem on the alien mahogany desk. I turned on the boom box. *Rosenkavalier* was just ending. A concerto for cello was announced, composed by a certain Monn. A cello. My favorite instrument. Curiously, I listened. When the cello's deepest tones sounded the thought occurred that it's true: the cello's sounds are the sounds of death.

If I knew music I think I would not be as surprised as I am by its resemblance to literature, especially by the recurrent themes and motifs in both. With this difference: in good literature those themes and motifs morph into ideals. but I don't feel that happening in music. Except … well, there is the cello and death. Reminds me of water. I look out the window to make sure the rain is still there. The motifs, the objects and settings, the situations and structures lurking behind the theme symbolize an idea which *could* become an ideal, toward which goal the creator with his narrative theme strives. Such motifs are the landmarks in music and in literature … as well as in my life. Sometimes in music it seems so simple: I listen to Rachmaninoff's Piano Concerto and wait until the nostalgia theme returns, and I sing the pop song's words under my breath, "full moon and empty arms" and smile to myself. Then, immediately after arrives the regret.

I pick up the picture of her and hold it at eye level. Only twenty-nine months. Gone. A mistake to look at it. The panic, pure, unadulterated panic sweeps over me. Like a sledge hammer it hits my stomach. Up my legs creeps the familiar weakness. The invaders are back. Over-breathing. Desperation. What can I do, alone? Only an internal explosion can end it. The only way it will ever stop. The emergency exit. Cello death. Nastya, oh, Anastasia. All-of-a-piece Nastya can talk it away. She never fails. She talks, quietly, quietly. Or she imparts the simplicity of eloquent silence, the silence of luxuriant forests, the silence I suspect she nourishes in secret. With her words she turns off the deadly timer of my uncommunicative diffidence. Pulls me out of whatever obscure pit I fall into when under attack. I listen to her imaginary talk. And slowly *it* ebbs away.

Once it struck me at a sidewalk café in front of the Church of the Madeleine: 'Back to the hotel, Nastya,' I mumbled, 'gotta get backonto the bed have to find a position have to search have to do it have to try have to lie down have to walk have to breathe softly slowly have to stop this fast breathing. Call a doctor, Nastya, call a doctor. Have to have to have to. Find a position. Yes, on my side like that, legs curled, fetal position.'

Again Nastya talked. At the café just opposite the Madeleine.

'No, no, gotta' get up. Gotta get out of here. Back outside. Cancel the doctor! Have to walk. Gotta get out of here. Back to the café. Observe the Madeleine. Watch the traffic.'

And Nastya talked. Held my hands in both hers, asked questions and talked.

'It was so cruel,' I insisted. 'Or much more. Providence's

punishment. Yes, yes, she's gone forever. No, no, nothing I can do to bring her back. She is no more … only in me.'

The talking helped. The monster in me shifted positions, uncertainly. I felt it. It retreated slowly, ever so slowly, back down my legs and away. But I felt its presence nearby. It hovered over me like buzzards over a dead animal in the Mohave. It lurked there, lurking. But outside me.

She too was terrified, there at the Madeleine. And so she talked. She always succeeded. Then when I walked around the table, beginning to feel free of *it* and whole again, Nastya ordered: "Talk!"

And I talked, there in front of the Madeleine. I told her about the psychiatrist who suggested the pain came from my Protestant heritage, that in reality I didn't consider her death an act of Fate but that of a vengeful God punishing a disobedient child.

'Was he right, Nastya? Was he right? Everything seems linked. You know what I mean?'

I was not supposed to forget, the shrink admitted. But I had to come to terms with the pain. It was mine. The pain that had transformed into this *thing*, this dissolute and unpredictable barometer-monster; creeping up and down along the dark corridors of my legs and psyche, into other corridors straight to my stomach and heart.

'I'm alone, that fake Freudian said. Alone, Nastya. I had to fight alone my fragility, my terrors, my anxiety and panic attacks, my claustrophobia, my timidity, yes, my insecurity and the awareness that I am who I am, he said, and that I have to live with me. Still, today, Nastya, I live with me. With you, too. Anastasia, I… I … need you.'

But the eternal question remains: Is mourning never complete? Or is mine not real mourning … but self-pity. Or do my manias, my pain my inability to accept that she is gone forever, does it all result from a refusal to accept the finality of death?

And so, talking and making love, I fell in love with Nastya over and over. I, who once walking across the campus at a great university, girls giggled at me in my Irish woolens and tan topcoat. I was a playboy, they whispered. I died of chagrin. I looked at myself in the hotel room mirror and vowed to get rid of all the new woolens. It was 1990. They still needed warm clothes in Russia. Nastya sent it all to Leningrad.

5.

Rumors continued to circulate. Playboy Monty! Sports cars, flashy lifestyle, flashy women. My life came to be measured by before Nastya time and since Nastya time. Days were work, late afternoons and weekends the children. And nights, Nastya.

Still, the mark of Cain was upon me. So when the President invited me to a private lunch, I knew it was all over, like General Paulus knew Germany had lost the war when the Red Army defeated his Sixth Army at Stalingrad.

After drinks and compliments on my achievements, he got to the point. So off-handedly, so mildly, that at first I hardly perceived where he was leading me. A short-lived deception it was.

'Now Montgomery, you know how we appreciate you here. Despite your terrible personal loss back then which saddened us all, your advancement has been meteoric. Back in my early days things moved according to a much slower rhythm, more methodical, more hierarchical.'

Hierarchical? That was not me. I knew then for sure that the axe was about to fall.

'But not everyone understands you. Now voices have reached me, er, Montgomery, critical voices which we cannot ignore, considering the sensitive nature of our cultural and—I must underline—moral tasks. You can appreciate our point of view. The Board agrees that the situation must be, er, remedied. The opinion is that for your own well-being you should normalize, I mean to say you should, er, harmonize your personal affairs with your position. We all, Board, managers and general staff, think highly of your beautiful family and truly wish for your sakes a restoration of the serenity of your former family relations. Otherwise, Montgomery, it is, umm, impossible for me to forecast future Board actions.'

The die was cast. The President and his mythical Board had laid down the law: get your shit together or you are the ex-youngest ever Operations Director. So I should patch a family life back together, return home and abandon Nastya … or I was out. Out of a lifestyle, out, out, out. Still on the opposite riverbank.

What to do? As Camus wrote, it's not easy to become what we are. And hard to find again our most profound measure. There where the truth counts. Always the truth. Is that a limit? I wonder, eyeing the Old Man with profound distaste.

The next day we were departing for the South. A work vacation. And the time of decision. To choose between Nastya and love and a failed family for whom I had to provide. Or choose not to choose and let the chips fall where they may.

We saw the majestic Dolomites, we admired *The Last Supper,* we commented on the *Davide* and we walked crossed the Ponte Vecchio. We took the ferry for a lunch on Ischia knowing all the time the end was near.

We drove back home at night. In the early morning hours Nastya curled on the seat with her head in my lap. The last eighty kilometers, as the first pink light rose from the East Nastya took me in her mouth and while I stroked her golden hair she held me until we reached home.

It was good-bye. During our drive she had spoken with compassionate doubt of my belief that I could live a decent life in this situation. She would return to her home country; I back to my ....

The present collapsed. But one thing remained. Duplicity remained in me. As did my desperation at the reality of losing the great love of my life. However, I didn't reveal to her the real reason for my return 'home': the President's edict.

Nor did I reveal that factor to my wife either when we agreed to try again for the sake of our children. Double deception.

And now a bleak reality for me remains—the President and the mystical Board, my job and the detestable mahogany desk, the dark river and the unrelenting rain notwithstanding. Who is going to talk away the monster in me now?

Absurd my presumption that I could have it all. Now I have to live for the rest of my life with the consequences of my cowardice ... or my prudence. And I hang onto the hope that I will never get used to mahogany desks.

The End.

OTHER WORKS BY GAITHER STEWART

Novels:

The Trojan Spy
Lily Pad Roll
Time of Exile
The Fifth Sun
Asheville
The Three Russians – a novella and a short story – Kindle edition

Short Story Collections:

Once in Berlin
To Be A Stranger
Icy Current, Compulsive Cours
Voices From Pisaloca

Essays:

Recollection of Things Learned—Remembering Socialism
Babylon Falling

www.ingramcontent.com/pod-product-compliance
Ingram Content Group UK Ltd.
Pitfield, Milton Keynes, MK11 3LW, UK
UKHW041314190726
13845UKWH00025B/255

9 789388 319478